MANHATTAN CLASSIC

MANHATTAN CLASSIC

New York's Finest Prewar Apartments

GEOFFREY LYNCH

Principal photography by Evan Joseph and Mike Tauber

Princeton Architectural Press · New York

CONTENTS

MANHATTAN LOCATIONS

INTRODUCTION:
THE MANHATTAN PREWAR
APARTMENT HOUSE

For many New Yorkers, real estate is an obsession. Dinner-party discussions quickly turn to addresses, views, lobbies, and maintenance fees. It's an expensive and arduous struggle to find a home you love; the hunt involves walking through many apartments that are overpriced letdowns. You may find it difficult to suppress a surge of real estate envy when visiting friends' perfect new places, listening to their long stories about the lucky happy ending that occurred just after they had lost all hope of finding a home. We yearn for what we probably can't ever afford: one of those extraordinarily beautiful apartments we see in glossy magazines and real estate ads, flawlessly designed right down to the doorknobs—the trophy homes, photographed with celebrity owners who describe their regular jaunts to the Paris flea markets to find just the right side table.

Prewar apartment houses, constructed between 1870 and 1935, contain some of the most consistently desirable homes in the city. On average they cost significantly more than their newer counterparts; these great works of architectural design almost never come on the market because residents can't imagine leaving, except feet first. New York's prewars ignite extraordinary passion; living in a prewar designed by one of that era's celebrated architects in one of their best buildings is a priceless luxury, often marking a person's entry into high society.

Walking along Manhattan's Park Avenue or the streets of the Upper West Side, you may wonder how this passion for prewars originated. Though pleasant, their architecture is generally calm and unexceptional. A location on Fifth Avenue overlooking Central Park is impressive, but aren't they just nice apartment buildings?

If you have the opportunity, visit a few of these apartment homes for a firsthand look. Perched high above the noisy streets, filled with light, and sometimes commanding spectacular skyline views, prewars have come to define the elegance and glamour of living in New York City. They have the beauty, proportions, and elegance of private houses; prewars were deliberately designed to convince families to give up their town houses, matching or surpassing them architecturally while providing the luxuries of twenty-four-hour doormen and a dedicated superintendent. Some buildings even had a private dining room and chef facility. They are quiet, and the air is fresh and cool. Instead of the gritty city being on the other side of a thin wood front door, there's always a doorman or two watching the street for you. Near good schools, restaurants, museums, and all the city offers, they offer privacy, security, and stately architecture, with an almost obsessive attention to detail in the woodwork, fine wood floors, moldings, brass door handles, and many other handcrafted features.

The buildings' exteriors feature three-story walls of smooth, thick limestone slabs, topped by ten or more stories of simple brick in earth tones ranging from Indian red to dark brown to sandy beige. Reaching out to the curb is a regal deep blue or private-club-green canvas canopy to both announce the address and keep residents and visitors dry on rainy nights as they wait for cabs. Double-hung windows are centered in rows above a pair of small, heavy-looking, black latticed front doors. A doorman in a hat and uniform is waiting just behind the glass; a bit like a private club, it's designed to be hard to see inside. Though hundreds of people may live in the building, it's meant to feel secure and intimate, not grand like a hotel. Residents are greeted by a smile from someone who knows them by name. The door swings open, and they glide into a narrow room finished in smooth, warm marble and soft lighting, leaving the city behind.

If you've never been in a prewar apartment house, you may not be prepared for how expansive the rooms are. Their very height, with lofty ceilings accommodating large, sun-drenched windows, harks back to a luxury and grace lost in the practical approach to post–World War II apartment design. They really do seem like homes in the sky—particularly the duplexes, where visitors arrive from a private elevator that gives access to a grand, chandelier-lit foyer with a curving stair toward one end, opening into huge, perfectly proportioned public rooms with marble fireplaces and windows in just the right places. Three or four bedrooms are hidden upstairs. These treasures of urban domestic architecture were built during an era when elegance and comfort were paramount. They reflected an unspoken message about social class: separate service elevators and servants' quarters were the norm. Today, finding a prewar apartment in pristine condition is rare, as they either command stratospheric prices or have been subdivided into smaller one- and two-bedrooms, following the dictates of economic necessity. Whether large or small, however, these homes maintain their sense of grandeur and charm, making them highly coveted in the always-competitive Manhattan real estate market.

The center-hall floor plan is the defining architectural move of prewar apartments (which are typically categorized by number of rooms: a *classic six* has two bedrooms in addition to maid's quarters, and a *classic eight* has four bedrooms plus maid's quarters). For example, in a 1,600-square-foot classic six, such as an A-line home at 800 West End Avenue, the entrance is not through the public corridor beside the kitchen but through a remarkably sizable foyer, 28 feet long and 8 feet wide. There's a painting or two on the wall, and you, the tired city dweller, feel embraced by the space as you drop your keys in a dish on a wood sideboard, take off your shoes, and receive a welcome-home kiss. A tall, framed doorway opens onto a wide living room with a marble fireplace in the middle and two large windows centered on the wall facing the street. The living room is far enough from the front door that you don't hear your neighbor's television from across the hall. Through another framed doorway is a large dining room. Bedrooms are tucked away for privacy down a short hall. Ten-foot ceilings and windows in each room make spaces feel even bigger and brighter. Those hallmark prewar details are abundant: just the right baseboards; inlaid herringbone wood floors; cute, classic white tile bathrooms. Even closets, rare in modern apartments though so important to living in the city, are large and plentiful. Whoever designed this apartment clearly worked hard to make it feel like a real family home, where you'd feel proud to raise your children.

New York City has an extraordinarily rich portfolio of residential architecture dating from the latter half of the nineteenth century through the early 1930s. An astonishing amount of that was built in the 1920s construction frenzy leading up to the stock market crash of 1929. Some apartment houses reach for the sky along Central Park West, tempting buyers with dramatic, postcard-ready spires. Fifth Avenue, Park Avenue, and Riverside Drive, known for their penthouse apartment mansions, offer some of the finest residential architecture in the world. You'll quickly learn, however, that a lot of apartment houses don't have park views or high-wattage addresses, but instead can be found lining the avenues and the major cross streets, such as West Eighty-Sixth Street on the Upper West Side. Almost a hundred, totaling more square footage than the downtowns of most American cities, adorn the wide, tree-lined sidewalks of sleepy West End Avenue. More are below Fourteenth Street, and a few were built in Brooklyn Heights and Park Slope.

The apartment house got off to a slow start in New York as a French import in the 1860s. In elite social circles of that time, it was considered immoral for a well-off family to share the same roof with another family. Sharing even a town house divided into two duplexes would be a stain on a family's reputation. The apartment house had an image problem, as it was perceived to be too much like a tenement, those unadorned five- or six-story walk-up apartment buildings you still see today on, for example, Orchard Street on the Lower East Side. Tenements were once home to thousands of immigrant families of four or many more, crowded into tiny, airless two- or three-room apartments. Walls were paper-thin, and a communal bathroom was located out in the rear yard. The lot-line walls may have been brick, but the floors were all wood, making them noisy and prone to collapse and fire—a problem for town houses, too.

As the population of Manhattan soared over the next twenty years, developers and their architects designed more apartment houses. They carried out experiments with different floor plans, room proportions, facades, and architectural details in attempts to achieve the graciousness of a nineteenth-century house in a twelve-story building. Some, such as the Dakota at Seventy-Second Street and Central Park West, looked like grand hotels or overdecorated cakes. Floor plans in buildings constructed before about 1908 can be awkward, with all the rooms connected by one very long corridor. One major challenge was that these New York buildings were three

times as tall as the classic English and Italian architectural styles often drawn upon; their original exquisite proportions were stretched with mixed success.

Cast-iron structures and concrete floors eventually replaced wood and solid brick. Elevators were necessary to convince families to live above the third floor. These were the two key ingredients for making skyscrapers and represented the forefront of construction technology in the late 1800s. It was far more economical and less risky to erect a light steel frame and clad it in heavy-looking brick than it was to build solid brick walls three or four feet thick, nine stories tall. Far taller buildings with more apartments were suddenly possible; for the first time in history, buildings other than church domes reached more than about six stories. To attract families, they could be advertised as completely fireproof, very quiet, and full of the latest in modern appliances and conveniences. Twelve stories quickly became the default height until 1929, when the passage of New York's Multiple Dwelling Law allowed even taller apartment houses on large lots or wide streets.

By the early years of the twentieth century, around 1908 or 1909, the apartment house's image problem had begun to fade. Spectacular examples such as the Apthorp at West Seventy-Ninth Street and Broadway and the Belnord at West Eighty-Sixth Street and Broadway were proof to well-to-do families that an apartment house could be comparable to a town house. Instead of living in a mansion, they could inhabit part of a palace. At twelve stories and 665,000 square feet, covering an entire city block, the 800-foot-long Belnord must have seemed colossal when it opened in 1909, looming over adjacent row houses and blocking out their sun.

Just like today, luxury bathrooms and kitchens were the rage; apartments might feature porcelain tubs and pedestal lavatories, a porcelain-lined refrigerator, or a laundry room with steam-jet washtubs for boiling clothes. For a rapidly growing country, these big, modern buildings represented the future and a sense of relentless optimism.

New York was growing at an astonishing pace, expanding from five hundred thousand inhabitants in 1850 to almost five million by 1910. Between 1890 and 1900, the population more than doubled. Where were all these people going to live? As brand-new subway lines branched out to the far ends of the city for the first time, making it easy to get from uptown to Wall Street in thirty minutes, apartment house construction boomed. Families could live a short walk from all the greenery and fresh air of Central Park, work downtown, and not spend long hours traveling between the two.

Construction slowed between the beginning of World War I and 1921 and took off again as the Roaring Twenties rocketed along. Entire neighborhoods seemingly tripled in height, as rows of four-story town houses were flattened to make way for fifteen-story apartment houses. Perhaps typical of economic boom cycles, many of the biggest, most spectacular architectural landmarks, such as 740 Park Avenue and 120 East End Avenue, were finished just as the economy dove into the Great Depression. When banks stopped lending money to developers, new construction ground to a halt. Like a delicate tree that thrives in just the right conditions of sunlight, temperature, and rain and then vanishes completely when its climate changes, the prewar building era was over.

By that point, the great fifty-year apartment house boom had transformed the architectural landscape of the city, pumping enormous energy into its already vibrant street life. Thousands of very desirable apartments were within a short walk or subway ride of restaurants, theaters, and museums; the Upper East Side continues to have the highest population density in the United States. But starting in the 1930s, as more families could afford cars, New York's suburbs overtook the city as the place to live. Few luxurious family-size apartments—the ones you really want from the moment you walk through the front door—would be built again until the first decade of the twenty-first century, during another real estate boom.

The architects who designed these buildings have largely been forgotten by history, although even today, their names act as precious keywords that help apartment seekers navigate the aggressive and baffling world of Manhattan real estate. *Bing & Bing* means very good. *Candela* seems to mean the best. These developers and architects played a crucial role shaping the streetscapes

of the city's best neighborhoods and establishing New York as a global center for fine architecture.

Often, prewar architects were self-taught, first-generation immigrants who couldn't afford to go to architecture school. Instead, they learned their trade on the job as apprentices. Long hours were spent bent over drafting tables, crafting center-hall plans and brick facades. Their clients were developers who were struggling to keep up with the city's phenomenal growth, including the Campagna family, Dwight P. Robinson & Company, the Paterno Construction Company, and Jacqueline Kennedy Onassis's grandfather, James T. Lee.

These architects were shunned by the established architectural community, whose members (drawn from wealthy families) had often studied for years at the grand École des Beaux Arts in Paris, been sent on long architectural tours of Europe, and built portfolios of grand mansions and public buildings. Emery Roth, who designed the towering San Remo and the monumental Beresford on Central Park West, was rejected in his first membership application to the American Institute of Architects in 1927.

Rosario Candela, a Sicilian immigrant, was the master of the center-hall floor plan and transformed his buildings' facades into highly refined, majestic compositions, often blending well-proportioned Italian details with dramatic tapering forms. Over the years, the name *Candela* has in one word come to identify the city's finest prewars. (A classic six in Candela's 800 West End Avenue, on the corner of Ninety-Ninth Street near Riverside Park, was what first drew me to prewars.) His great apartment houses, such as 740 and 778 Park Avenue and 834 Fifth Avenue, are almost impossible to get into, even for those able to afford their stratospheric prices.

Other prominent prewar architects include J. E. R. Carpenter, whose work is concentrated on Fifth and Park Avenues and shows remarkable restraint. His finest building may be the dramatic, Gothic-inspired, curving 173–175 Riverside Drive, across the street from the Soldiers' and Sailors' Monument in Riverside Park. Schwartz & Gross was the architecture firm that set the warm, yet proud, masonry tone of West End Avenue, Central Park West, and Park Avenue. Their firm designed hundreds of apartment houses that established the family-friendly architectural fabric of the Upper West

Side and Upper East Side. Brothers George and Edward Blum were more eccentric, experimenting with ornate terra-cotta ornament such as the unexpected all-white, art nouveau facade of 780 West End Avenue and the bold, brightly colored zigzags of Gramercy House on East Twenty-Second Street. Around Columbia University, you'll find many of Gaetano Ajello's buildings, which were built during the first dense waves of apartment house construction on the Upper West Side. Also prolific were George F. Pelham and Rouse & Goldstone.

Of course, the great civic architects of early twentieth-century New York contributed a few extraordinary apartment houses. McKim, Mead & White created the palatial 998 Fifth Avenue and a few others on Park Avenue, since replaced with much larger office buildings. Warren & Wetmore designed both 927 Fifth Avenue and 903 Park Avenue (though the firm focused on monumental stone piles such as Grand Central Station and the Farley Post Office rather than the aggressive profit-driven realm of residential development).

There were many others. Yet it is important to emphasize that although the luxurious buildings on Fifth and Park Avenues or Central Park West garner most of the attention, the great prewar architects also designed hundreds of more modest and attainable buildings that nonetheless enjoy the warmth and gracious style of their fabulous cousins. Robert T. Lyons, best known for his palatial Park Avenue apartments, retooled what he learned there on a less opulent scale at 535 West 110th Street, near Broadway and Columbia University. If you like Emery Roth's work, there are nine of his buildings on West End Avenue alone, as well as eleven by Candela. In fashion terms, they are the ready-to-wear collections styled after luxury brands.

The apartment houses in this book are curated highlights of the thousands you'll find in Manhattan. Together, they illustrate the building type's brief history and architectural evolution, from its roots in an elite, borrowed, nineteenth-century Parisian way of living to its flowering as an unmistakably glamorous form of New York skyscraper in the early 1930s, more desirable to the rich than a private mansion.

A NOTE TO THE READER

This book represents examples of apartment houses from each Manhattan neighborhood and major street. Brief histories accompany a number of the more renowned and well-documented buildings; detailed information such as who designed each of the buildings on Park Avenue can be found in the two indexes, organized by neighborhood and by architect. Buyers who are determined to live in a Candela or Roth or Bing & Bing building should search there. (Although every effort has been made to confirm the accuracy of these listings, sometimes existing sources contain conflicting information.)

Each building entry highlights an exemplary floor plan, meticulously redrawn (at a scale of 1 inch = 20 feet, unless otherwise noted) and paired with beautiful color photography of one or more noteworthy additional apartments that show how the great prewar idea is lived and experienced more than one hundred years after its inception.

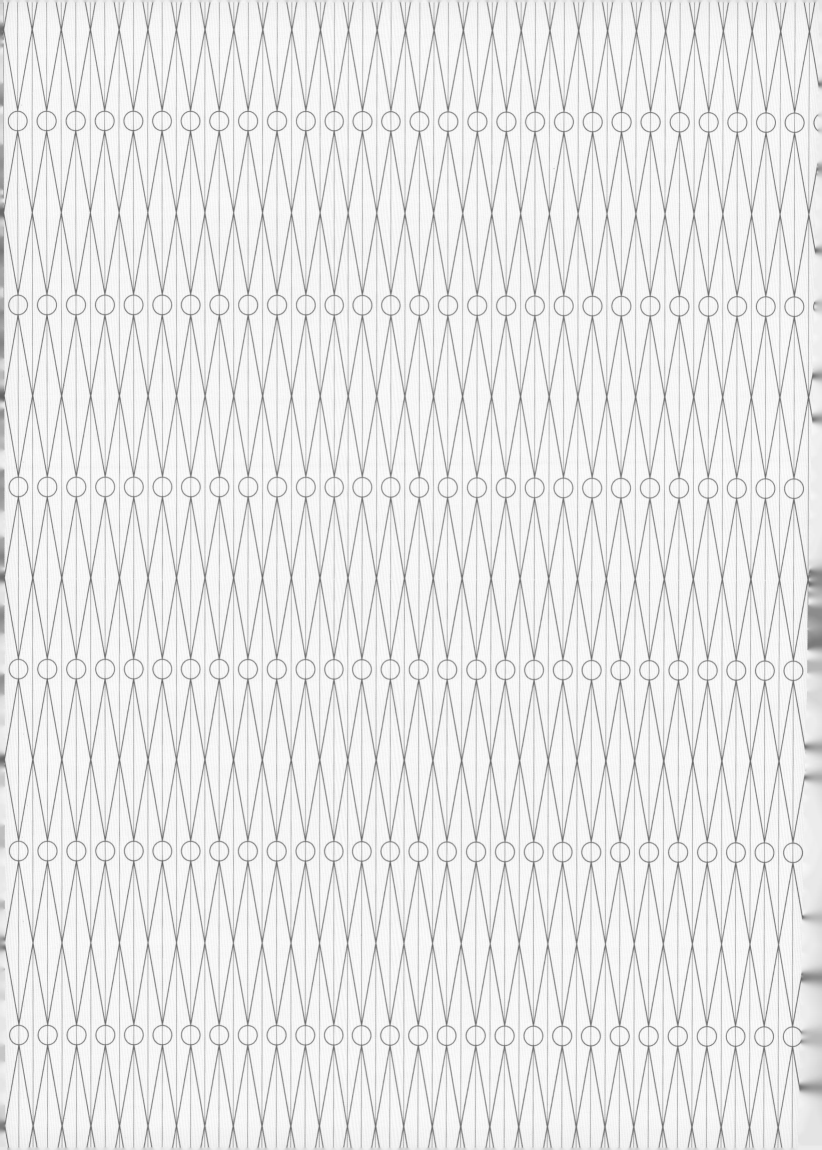

UPPER EAST SIDE: FIFTH AVENUE

810 FIFTH AVENUE

820 FIFTH AVENUE

Considered by some the finest apartment house on Fifth Avenue, and one of the most expensive addresses in the world, 820 Fifth Avenue is an all-cash, white-glove building, where being a billionaire is no guarantee of making it past the co-op board or even getting an interview.

The building, on the northeast corner of Sixty-Third Street, was developed by the Paterno Construction Company. Prolific builders noted for their apartment houses in Morningside Heights, around Columbia University, Paterno also built the imposing 440 Riverside Drive, 825 and 856 Fifth Avenue, and 1220 Park Avenue.

Paterno hired architecture firm Starrett & Van Vleck, best known for its high-end department stores, including the Lord & Taylor building on Fifth Avenue between Thirty-Eighth and Thirty-Ninth Streets, recently completed in 1914. At first Starrett & Van Vleck seemed to be an odd

choice, but given that its existing work catered to the rich, the firm knew the spaces in which the wealthy felt comfortable. It mastered the center-hall plan in one go at a time when that convention was still emerging. Oddly, 820 would be Starrett & Van Vleck's only apartment house.

The building includes only twelve homes—two maisonettes and ten full-floors—which are rarely sold and never officially put on the market. The fifth-floor apartment has some 7,500 square feet, nine windows facing Central Park, and eighteen rooms, including five bedrooms, six and one-half bathrooms, and a 44-foot-long gallery ideal for entertaining. There are two manned elevators. For privacy in a very nosy city, a driveway is paired with a waiting room for chauffeurs, allowing residents to come and go unnoticed.

Publicity-shy residents have included Louise Crane of the Crane & Company stationery family; prominent secondary-art-market dealer William Acquavella, whose gallery is in a limestone mansion on East Seventy-Ninth Street; and billionaire Kenneth Griffith, who founded the hedge fund Citadel Investment Group in Chicago.

McKim, Mead & White's masterpiece 998 Fifth Avenue, completed four years earlier, had set a high bar; 820 was deliberately similar in plan, size, and grandeur. Its all-limestone, heavily rusticated neo–Italian Renaissance facade looks massive, eternal, and fortresslike. Exhibiting tremendous architectural restraint, yet exuding a clear sense of civic power and permanence, the building features seventh-floor balconies that seem designed to serve as a platform for some important public official. J. E. R Carpenter's 907 Fifth Avenue, finished the same year, is stylistically akin.[1]

834 FIFTH AVENUE

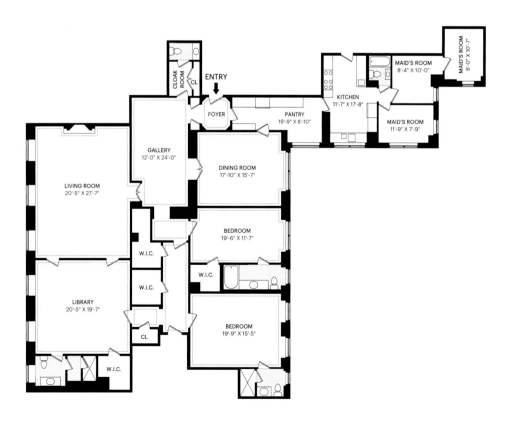

A resident of 834 Fifth Avenue once asked, "Why would you move out of 834 unless you've died?"[2]

Developer Anthony Campagna tried unsuccessfully for two years to buy all six town houses along the blockfront between Sixty-Fourth and Sixty-Fifth Streets, but the corners remained holdouts. Moving ahead, he hired Rosario Candela (after having worked with him on 960 Fifth Avenue) to design a symmetrical, tapering, sixteen-story superluxury apartment house, one that would break out of the mold of the cornice-topped palazzo that had been firmly established by 998 Fifth Avenue at its completion in 1912. Here would be a skyscraper further refining designs Candela already had underway for nearby apartment houses at 720, 740, 770, and 778 Park Avenue—exuberant architecture reflecting the bubble of the 1920s economic boom, dotted with terraces and featuring spectacular duplex and triplex penthouses that were unquestionably mansions in the sky.

The building ended up asymmetrical when Margaret V. Haggin capitulated after construction started and sold her town house on the corner of Sixty-Fourth Street to Campagna. Completed in 1931 after two years of construction, the 187,000-square-foot structure had twenty-four palatial homes with sizes ranging from 4,000 to 7,000 square feet, including two maisonettes and several spectacular duplexes.

Stockbrokerage kingpin Charles Schwab had a penthouse. Bing Crosby's son Harry lived in one of the maisonettes. *Phantom of the Opera* producer Hal Prince had a home there. Leslie Wexner, president and CEO of Limited Brands, moved there from an 18,000-square-foot Stanford White–designed town house at 25 East Seventy-Eighth Street. In 1948 Laurance S. Rockefeller hired the architecture firm Harrison & Abramovitz, later known for the corporate office towers it designed in the 1950s and 1960s, to create a sprawling triplex penthouse, now the home of News Corporation founder Rupert Murdoch.

Apartment 3/4C has huge public rooms for entertaining. A 31-foot-long entry gallery framing a grand curved stair opens to a living room and library facing Central Park, bookended by marble fireplaces. Combined, the rooms are almost 60 feet long. Higher up, above the park's treetops in the 4,750-square-foot 13/14A, a private elevator landing opens onto a double-height foyer facing a grand circular stair. To the right is a 19-by-29-foot living room centered on a dramatic fireplace, beyond which is a library with its own terrace facing the park and midtown. Upstairs, both the master bedroom and master bath also face the park.

This all-limestone building overlooking the Central Park Zoo is one of the most desirable on the avenue and one of Candela's finest.

907 FIFTH AVENUE

ENTRY

CL

FOYER
12'-5" X 13'-6"

OFFICE
7'-6" X 22'-6"

SCREENING ROOM
18'-4" X 19'-9"

LIBRARY
21'-0" X 21'-6"

CL CL

W.I.C.

CL CL

AUX. KITCHEN
17'-0" X 8'-0"

WET BAR

GALLERY
12'-0" X 23'-0"

DINING ROOM
23'-6" X 13'-6"

KITCHEN
8'-9" X 21'-0"

BEDROOM
13'-8" X 9'-4"

CL

CL CL CL

CL CL

CL

LIVING ROOM
21'-3" X 30'-9"

CL

BEDROOM
13'-3" X 14'-6"

CL CL

CL

BREAKFAST
ROOM
9'-0" X 12'-2"

W/D

BEDROOM
14'-0" X 15'-0"

MASTER BEDROOM
14'-8" X 18'-0"

DRESSING AREA
10'-8" X 8'-4"

CL

Before getting the commission for 907, his first building on Fifth Avenue, J. E. R. Carpenter had nurtured his hand designing three luxury apartment houses on Park Avenue. Stately, all-brick 960, with a twelve-room and a ten-room home on each floor, was completed in 1912 for Fullerton Weaver Realty. He would later repeat this model at 550 and 950 Park Avenue. Two more apartment houses for the same client at 635 and 640 Park Avenue would soon follow. This time the apartments were huge full-floors, where he further explored the center-hall plan and experimented with the size of the foyer and the relationship of the public rooms to the avenue outside.

The twelve-story 907 Fifth Avenue, a limestone-clad Italian Renaissance palazzo on the southeast corner of busy Seventy-Second Street, would be the first apartment house north of Fifty-Seventh Street to replace a private

mansion—James A. Burden's barely twenty-year-old pile designed by Robert Henderson (R. H.) Robertson. The new building would have twenty-two homes, most with two twelve-room apartments per floor, comprising 147,000 square feet and posing a confrontational change in scale for the avenue.

When 907 was completed in 1916, the top floor was rented by Herbert L. Pratt, a Standard Oil vice president (whose Glen Cove, Long Island, estate The Braes would later become the Webb Institute of Naval Architecture). Another legendary resident was publicity-shy Huguette Clark, heiress of the copper baron William Andrews Clark. Considered the country's second-richest man (behind only John D. Rockefeller) in 1900, William Andrews Clark built an opulent, outrageously ornate mansion for his family on the corner of Seventy-Seventh Street and Fifth Avenue.

In 1925, when he died, it was torn down to make way for Rosario Candela's 960 Fifth Avenue, and Huguette Clark moved to the twenty-eight-room penthouse at 907, which she owned for more than eighty years.

The penthouse's public rooms facing the park are by all means magnificent, though Clark rarely used them. The gallery off the elevator is 55 feet long. Two doorways open up to a 40-by-20-foot drawing room next to a 40-foot-long living room and, at the other end, a 30-foot-long library—a residential scale that's hard to imagine and that doesn't even include the dining room. Clark also maintained vast estates in Santa Barbara, California, and New Canaan, Connecticut. At the time of her death in 2011 at the age of 104, Clark was one of the last links to the city's prewar heyday; she willed much of her estate away to charity.[3]

960 FIFTH AVENUE

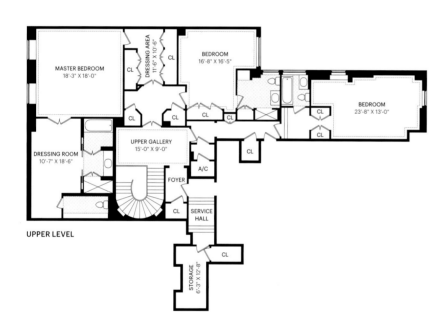

UPPER LEVEL

- MASTER BEDROOM 18'-3" X 18'-0"
- DRESSING AREA 11'-6" X 10'-6"
- BEDROOM 16'-8" X 16'-5"
- BEDROOM 23'-8" X 13'-0"
- DRESSING ROOM 10'-7" X 18'-6"
- UPPER GALLERY 15'-0" X 9'-0"
- FOYER
- A/C
- SERVICE HALL
- STORAGE 6'-3" X 12'-8"
- CL

LOWER LEVEL

- LIVING ROOM 29'-4" X 18'-2"
- DINING ROOM 17'-10" X 17'-0"
- STAFF 11'-10" X 9'-9"
- GALLERY 21'-0" X 8'-6"
- PANTRY
- KITCHEN 18'-5" X 15'-3"
- LIBRARY 17'-0" X 16'-6"
- LAUNDRY
- STAFF 10'-9" X 10'-10"
- ENTRY

If ever there was an architectural career that took off like a rocket, it was Rosario Candela's. Not only a prolific artist, Candela, perhaps more than any prewar architect, was the master of the glamorous luxury apartment house.

By the time 960 Fifth Avenue opened in 1928, Candela had designed forty-five apartment houses in six years, which gives some idea of the crazed speed at which New York was being rebuilt. His commissions' locations had also begun to shift at an astonishing scale, from mostly the west side of Central Park to Fifth and Park Avenues.

One of two mansions demolished to clear the site for 960 belonged to copper baron William Andrews Clark (see page 29). Clark's goal when he moved to New York in 1895 had been to build the largest and most expensive house in America. It took him a painful thirteen years to construct the 121 rooms and cost him an astonishing seven million dollars—about one hundred sixty-five million dollars today. More gingerbread house than architecture, it was completed in 1908, yet lasted only until 1925, when it was demolished by the new building's developer, Anthony Campagna.

Also known as 3 East Seventy-Seventh Street, 960's homes are an architecturally stunning mix of unique half-floors, duplexes, and simplexes with double-height living rooms, ranging from six to fourteen rooms apiece. Partnering with Warren & Wetmore, Candela developed floor plans to fit sixty-eight homes into a complex fifteen-story 3D puzzle, even making space for a private restaurant for residents, named the Georgian Suite.

The thirteen-room duplex 5/6B is hard to distinguish from a nineteenth-century mansion. Large public rooms wrap the entry foyer, whose focus is a grand, curved stair in front of a double-height curved wall. Upstairs are five bedrooms, including a massive master suite. Windows are unusually large, extending almost to the floor. Smaller but still vast classic sixes, such as 11A/B or 13C/D, received the same attention to grace, elegance, and detail. Residents of 960 have included Canadian liquor tycoon Edgar Bronfman, former Goldman Sachs vice chairman Roy J. Zuckerberg, and Venezuelan billionaire and media mogul Gustavo Cisneros.

Perhaps as homage to Clark's demolished mansion, 960 has no cornice. In its place is an unexpectedly Gothic row of hooded stone gargoyles, mythical figures looking down to the street with their eyes hidden and hands clasped together, watching the city as if silently protecting the building's residents and warning away any lurking urban evil.

998 FIFTH AVENUE

At the turn of the twentieth century, McKim, Mead & White was the go-to firm for exceedingly refined classical civic buildings and fabulous mansions. Architects to New York's elite, the company left an astonishing legacy of landmarks that the young city desperately needed to establish its international credentials, from the Municipal Building by City Hall to the stately University Club on Fifth Avenue, the Century Club, the Harvard Club, the Brooklyn Museum, and Columbia University's beautiful campus in Morningside Heights. Even after partner Stanford White was shot and killed by his lover's husband in 1906 and partner Charles Follen McKim died in 1909, their firm soldiered on to design the original Pennsylvania Station, the equally imperial-size James A. Farley Post Office Building across Eighth Avenue, and Adelphi University in Garden City, New York.

Apartment house architecture before World War I was in need of the legitimacy and sophistication to attract society's elite members. What type of building would convince some of the country's richest families to live under the same roof? Classical models from all over Europe, where buildings rarely topped six floors, were being adapted to buildings stretching to fifteen floors, with decidedly mixed results. Bases were rusticated stone. Cornice lines were scaled up. But what to do with the facade of all those additional floors in between? How much ornament? Usually far too much was applied, and with a heavy hand.

For what would be one of the first apartment houses on the gilded stretch of Fifth Avenue facing Central Park, the architecture needed to be palatial. The developer of 998 Fifth Avenue was James T. Lee, who would later build the equally extravagant 740 Park Avenue. Along with Charles L. Fleischmann, he had bought from August Belmont a site on the northeast corner of Eighty-First Street, across the street from the Metropolitan Museum of Art. He would use high design, at almost limitless expense, to convince mansion owners to move in. By the building's completion in 1912, Lee had spent lavishly, to the tune of almost $250,000 a floor— the same amount most developers spent on an entire building.[4]

The building featured modern luxuries such as a "central vacuum-cleaning system, jewelry and silver safes anchored in the walls of each apartment, remote laundries with ventilated steam-drying devices, basement storage rooms, refrigerated wine cellars and additional servants' quarter."[5] The rent for each home topped $25,000 a year.

The original handsome, substantial marquee over the Eighty-First Street entrance still exists, although it has lost some of its decorative elements. The formal lobby is mostly hidden from the street for privacy. Polished Italian marble walls and Tennessee marble floors lead to elevators lined in French walnut panels.

Upstairs, the imposing scale of the homes matched the opulent architectural tone of the facade. Public rooms were unquestionably grand, and foyers reached almost 40 feet long, divided by immense doors framed in marble. Designed as some of the most formal prewar floor plans in the city were eleven enormous full-floor homes with seventeen rooms each, as well as maisonettes, duplexes, and smaller simplexes.

Lee's costly bet on 998 Fifth worked. Within twenty years, most of the Fifth Avenue mansions that had been built to last for centuries had fallen like dominoes to make way for the wall of striking limestone apartment houses that still frame Central Park today.

1020 FIFTH AVENUE

LIVING ROOM
20'-1" X 42'-8"

DINING ROOM
17'-4" X 20'-6"

BEDROOM
11'-7" X 12'-7"

STAFF ROOM
13'-10" X 5'-8"

KITCHEN
18'-0" X 16'-11"

GALLERY
11'-3" X 16'-10"

← ENTRY

ELEV

ELEV

DRESSING ROOM

DRESSING ROOM

LIBRARY
18'-6" X 17'-1"

W.I.C.

BEDROOM
13'-1" X 17'-7"

BEDROOM
16'-2" X 17'-7"

MASTER BEDROOM
21'-7" X 15'-5"

CL

Warren & Wetmore is best known as the architect of Grand Central Station. Yet the firm's lesser-known apartment houses (927 and 1020 Fifth Avenue and 903 Park Avenue) are no doubt in the same elite tier as buildings designed by Candela and Carpenter. These three slender high-luxury buildings sit on small lots, permitting the exceedingly hard-to-get full-floor homes within.

A sumptuous townhouse built by Gilded Age banker William A. Salomon on the northeast corner of Eighty-Third Street was purchased by the prolific Paterno family of developers after his death and demolished in order to start construction.

The building, which faces south and west, occupies a prime location opposite the Metropolitan Museum of Art. The irregular window pattern on its limestone facade provides a hint of what makes six of the thirteen homes so desirable: double-height

living rooms facing Central Park. With an imperial-size fireplace at one end, each 20-by-40-foot room is ideal for entertaining and showing off. There are also three-bedroom duplexes, where the entry foyer has its own balcony overlooking Eighty-Third Street, next to a grand sweeping stair. Yet it's the triplex penthouse of noble proportions, originally owned by businessman Samuel H. Kress, that firmly established the building's prestige.

Kress built his fortune starting a five-and-dime competitor to Woolworth's. His stores throughout the country were known for their architecture. As his wealth grew, he invested in what would become the country's largest private collection of Italian Renaissance paintings. Working with famed art dealer Joseph Duveen, he amassed an almost encyclopedic collection of more than three thousand pieces. Gathering a mix of baroque

and old masters, he took advantage of the low prices for paintings from an era that had fallen out of fashion.

Around the time Kress moved into 1020 Fifth Avenue in 1925, he began to give his collection away to the American public. More than four hundred pieces were donated in 1941, along with works from a number of other benefactors, to found the National Gallery of Art in Washington, DC. Kress's collection was spread among eighteen museums around the country in cities where he had stores. In 1929 the Kress Foundation was founded to "share the artistic legacy of Europe with the American people."[6]

Kress's philanthropy exemplifies how Fifth Avenue's rapid shift toward a much more discreet architecture in the late 1920s, away from outrageous architectural displays of wealth, occurred in parallel with New York's growing cultural maturity and prominent position on the international stage.

1030 FIFTH AVENUE

1170 FIFTH AVENUE

UPPER EAST SIDE: PARK AVENUE

417 PARK AVENUE

Before World War II, Park Avenue south of Fifty-Ninth Street was lined with luxury apartment houses. In the decades after the war, all but two were demolished to make way for hulking glass office buildings. The real estate was just too valuable to be built only fifteen stories tall, especially as the properties were a short walk from Grand Central Station, permitting an easy commute for the morning mass of office workers and executives coming from suburbs in upstate New York and Connecticut. The elegant 417 Park Avenue was one of the two apartment houses spared.

Though it is smaller than most of Emery Roth's apartment houses, thirteen-story 417 Park is one of his most handsome. Roth got the classical details just right, to the point where if it weren't so tall, the building could be mistaken for being five hundred years old, a Renaissance artifact imported in pieces.

Roth had been designing apartment houses since 1899, the year after he bought a small two-person firm to start his architectural practice. His clients for 417 Park were the Bing brothers, Leo and Alexander. At the time, like Roth, they were building a business; theirs had opened in 1906, and they were experimenting with what would make their buildings competitive within the tide of apartment houses sweeping over Manhattan. Bing & Bing buildings would become desirable for their wide rooms, step-down living rooms, and ample closet space. Eventually, Bing & Bing would build more than forty rental apartment houses, and not only ones in the superluxury category. Bing & Bing became a brand, like Candela and Carpenter, coveted by real estate aficionados.

Completed in 1916, 417 Park consists of only twenty-eight units, with typically two classic eights to a floor—east and west—served by two elevator cores opening onto private foyers. There are four penthouses, two of which are duplexes. The facade is all limestone, resembling a stretched, yet noticeably formal palazzo, and a massive copper-clad cornice hangs well over the sidewalk below. The spare use of powerful classical stone details against the otherwise flat, light-gray facade marks the building's character, just as a great painting displays a skillful balance of color and light. As you turn the corner down leafy East Fifty-Fourth Street toward the building's extraordinarily intimate front entrance, with doors just tall enough to walk through, you are transported in a few steps from a modern corporate capital to a place that seems frozen nearly a century in the past.

580 PARK AVENUE

MAID'S ROOM
8'-9" X 8'-6"

DINING ROOM
17'-0" X 16'-2"

LIVING ROOM
24'-0" X 16'-2"

BAR

KITCHEN
15'-6" X 9'-6"

PANTRY

CL

GALLERY
9'-6" X 25'-0"

BEDROOM
19'-0" X 12'-0"

W.I.C.

FOYER

CL

MASTER BEDROOM
15'-0" X 19'-6"

ENTRY

DRESSING ROOM /
W.I.C.

On a rare 75-foot-deep lot spanning the whole blockfront between Sixty-Third and Sixty-Fourth Streets, 580 Park is fortunate at only fourteen stories tall to have city views and a notable amount of light. On the west, it overlooks town houses and their backyard treetops. Across the avenue, to the east, are two churches with distinct architectural features of their own. The Third Church of Christ, Scientist, which has the appearance of a Georgian town hall, is on the Sixty-Third Street corner. On the Sixty-Fourth Street corner, finished a year before 580, is the decidedly heavy, Gothic Central Presbyterian Church. The latter was built as a Baptist church, designed by Allen & Collens (the firm behind Riverside Church at 122nd Street and Riverside Drive), working with sculptor Henry C. Pelton. So massive are the buttresses that they seem as if they could hold up a nave two or three times the size of the church's own. Odd, too, are the two floors of support

space built on top of the nave in lieu of a soaring pitched roof.

Designed by J. E. R. Carpenter for both the Dwight P. Robinson Company and the now ubiquitous Douglas L. Elliman & Company, 580 Park Avenue had fifty-two homes when it opened in 1923. Its brochure listed the building shareholders' names to assure prospective residents that they would maintain their social status. The building's Italian Renaissance palazzo style is familiar architecturally except for its base, which seems more evocative of a fortified bank, with its block-long row of stone pilasters and—quite unexpectedly—an almost 6-foot-tall solid wall of granite at sidewalk level, as if Carpenter had paired the base of an office building with the shaft of an apartment house.

Two identical L-shaped buildings were built end-to-end in order to establish two separate and private street lobbies and accompanying elevator cores—a distinguishing

feature of many large apartment houses. Originally there were four homes per floor (each with either eight or nine rooms), so each elevator would thereby serve only two homes per floor. In the A-line nine-room homes, one entered via a generous 14-foot-diameter circular foyer facing east to the living room as well as west to the dining room—a layout allowing natural light almost all day and providing the feeling of a house with multiple exposures.

A 200-foot-long facade makes 580 one of the avenue's most prominent apartment houses, with big, black windows fit between strong, horizontal string courses at a scale that even the huge 1185 Park Avenue can't muster. Perhaps Carpenter was inspired by the Apthorp or the Belnord, enormous courtyard apartment houses across Central Park completed back-to-back in 1908 and 1909, both of which have come to be known as grand architectural works.

610 PARK AVENUE
MAYFAIR HOUSE

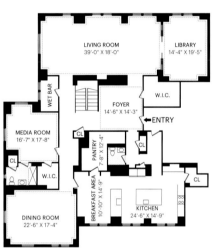

UPPER LEVEL

LOWER LEVEL

*Scale: 1"= 30'- 0"

640 PARK AVENUE

Apartment house architecture up until the 1920s usually aimed to conceal the fact that a light steel frame provided the building's structure, with a stone or brick facade acting only as a decorative weatherproof skin. Buildings still seemed massive and solid, with windows set far apart within thick walls, as European palazzos had been designed for hundreds of years. In part, these proportions were derived from the classical styles New York architects had adopted. But they were also a response to the public's uncertainty about the structural stability of a twelve-story building held up by steel sticks.

A flawless example of this style of building is 640 Park Avenue, an early work of J. E. R. Carpenter on the northwest corner of Sixty-Sixth Street. Across the street from the Park Avenue Armory, it was built by S. Fullerton Weaver, the real estate developer of architecture firm Schultze & Weaver, which also designed soaring Jazz Age

hotels, including the Pierre and the Sherry-Netherland in New York and the Breakers in Palm Beach.

Despite being only thirteen stories tall on a small lot, 640 has a palatial street presence. With narrow pairs of windows almost 10 feet apart, it appears to have been carved in place out of one colossal piece of limestone. Its huge, ornate cornice, another common characteristic of early apartment houses, only adds to its noble stature.

Its elegant full-floor homes, each with high ceilings and two enormous rooms facing the avenue, have attracted notable residents—Millard Drexel of global fashion chain J. Crew, former Lehman Brothers CEO Dick Fuld, and arts patron Evelyn Annenberg Jaffe Hall. A major donor to the Museum of Modern Art and the Memorial Sloan-Kettering Cancer Center, she was the sister of publisher Walter H. Annenberg, who started the hugely profitable *TV Guide* in 1952.[7]

655 PARK AVENUE

740 PARK AVENUE

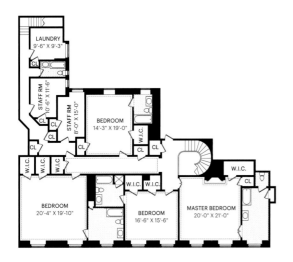

UPPER LEVEL

LOWER LEVEL

*Scale: 1" = 30'-0"

There are two of what could be called Park Avenue triumvirates straddling Seventy-Second Street: a total of six soaring, tapering apartment houses between Seventy-First and Seventy-Fourth Streets, reaching high above their flat-topped neighbors, all built in the brief construction froth after the 1929 stock market crash. Without question, Rosario Candela's four of these six buildings are where he cemented his reputation as the greatest of the prewar apartment house architects. The last few majestic apartment houses of that era raced to new heights of luxury, eventually concentrating some of the wealthiest New Yorkers in one four-block stretch.

These impressive structures capitalized on the new Multiple Dwelling Law of 1929. Residential architecture overnight shed its roots in the European palazzo, free from the box that had been dictated by the need to pack a building's total floor space within the previous height limit of 150 feet. A brand new form of modern urban castle appeared. Wedding-cake upper floors were shaped to maximize views and light for enormous penthouses and also to provide bay windows and terraces for grand rooms that had not been possible within a conventional box. Massing near the top was irregular—chamfered bay windows mingled with squared-off ones and with varying window sizes—because apartments were designed from the inside out. Forms were placed to benefit the proportions of rooms and their views rather than to create a perfectly proportioned facade.

Of the six, legendary 740, on the northeast corner of Seventy-First Street, is a coveted art deco architectural masterpiece that resembles a smooth limestone iceberg, glowing among its dark-brown brick neighbors. Almost entirely free of classical Italian ornament or even a cornice, its muscular beauty relies on its sculptural form, with a cascade of narrow terraces on Seventy-First Street facing the after-noon sun and a sliver view of the park, its fluted base and massive entryway framed by two solid granite columns. Cartouches just below the penthouse roofline provide hints of the Egyptian influences on art deco. Completed in 1930, the building was a radical architectural step forward, yet surprisingly refined in its application of the still-new art deco style.

On a 102-by-220-foot lot that would allow for dramatic floor plans, 740 was built by developer James T. Lee, who had established his luxury credentials as the developer of 998 Fifth Avenue. He was the grandfather of former First Lady Jacqueline Kennedy Onassis, who with her parents and younger sister Lee grew up a fixture of New York high society, living in 6/7A until her parents divorced.[8]

There are only thirty-one homes, which combined consume nineteen floors and 273,500 square feet. Each is remarkable, with ceilings that reach 13 feet. Many are duplexes with double-height foyers—impressive spaces for greeting dinner guests. The duplex 4/5C, for example, has a 35-foot-long entrance gallery with a grand curved stair. The living room is 36 by 20 feet and the library 18 by 20; a 25-by-20-foot dining room is well proportioned for entertaining. Four bedrooms and additional maids' rooms are located upstairs on the fifth floor, though by the late 1920s staff quarters were being built much smaller than they had been just fifteen years earlier.

The building opened in an economy in the midst of collapse and initially failed to attract wealthy buyers. It quickly was converted to a rental and, in 1953, to a co-op by John D. Rockefeller Jr. Michael Gross's tell-all book *740 Park Avenue: The World's Richest Apartment Building* lays out the building's glamorous history and striking list of famous and infamous residents, from Koch Industries billionaire David Koch to art collector and Neue Galerie founder Ronald Lauder to fashion designer Vera Wang.

Rockefeller himself lived there from 1937 to 1960 in the thirty-seven-room triplex on the fifteenth through seventeenth floors. Although it's known as the Rockefeller Apartment, the triplex was originally built for George and Eleanor Brewster. To be convinced to part with the mansion they had built in 1909 on that street corner, the Brewsters negotiated hard and were promised by James T. Lee that he would build them anything they wanted in the new building. George Brewster—whose ancestor William Brewster arrived on the *Mayflower*—brought instant credibility to the project.

Financier and art collector Saul Steinberg bought the triplex from the Rockefeller estate in 1971. Twenty-nine years later he sold it to Stephen Schwartzman, cofounder of the giant private equity firm Blackstone. Perhaps the city's largest apartment, the Rockefeller Apartment is a one-of-a-kind home for New York royalty.

760 PARK AVENUE

765/775 PARK AVENUE

778 PARK AVENUE

UPPER LEVEL

LOWER LEVEL

In 1929 Rosario Candela was at the top of his game. He was designing at full tilt; his office filed drawings for twenty-nine new luxury apartment houses with the city building department that year alone (although only about half would be finished, owing to the stock market crash). On March 13, 770 Park Avenue was filed. Two days later both 740 and 778 Park Avenue were filed.

This new breed of taller, tapered, light-filled apartment house topped by cascading terraces, at a scale allowed by the 1929 change in the zoning laws, represented the apex of the city's romance with the skyscraper mansion. If apartment house architecture had evolved effectively to radiate respectability and the understated elegance New York families sought, here was the siren in the shapely red dress, a creation of the city's phenomenal energy and ambition: the one-off home free to be shaped beyond the confines of the box.

Set on the northwest corner of Seventy-Third Street and Park Avenue, this nineteen-story English Renaissance building with eighteen homes was completed in 1931. Developer Charles Newmark ended up in foreclosure during construction, so the building was completed by another developer. An iconic neo-Georgian water-tank enclosure sits on the roof, framed by two Greek columns at each corner. Below, a jumble of bay windows, terraces, and tiny balconies look as though they were built over time, like an Italian hill town after centuries of progressive additions. A typical podium full-floor home had nine rooms and was entered via a 38-foot-long entrance gallery leading to three enormous public rooms facing the avenue.

It has been home to Vera Wang, cosmetics queen Estée Lauder, and former president of IBM Thomas J. Watson, though 778's fame comes primarily from two former residents: socialite and renowned philanthropist

Brooke Astor, who lived in a sixteen-room duplex on the fourteenth and fifteenth floors, and conservative icon William F. Buckley Jr., who, with his wife, Pat, lived in the one maisonette—a thirteen-room, 5,000-square-foot home with its own address, 73 East Seventy-Third Street.

As if shaking off historical constraints in order to express the vibrancy of life in New York, both of these celebrated residents bucked the decorating trend of muted tones in favor of glossy red lacquer and rich greens, creating some of the most dramatic rooms in any prewar. More an English country house in the sky than an apartment, the Astor home was full of light from French doors opening up onto terraces. The plan's grand rooms pivoted around the gallery, so that many had views in two directions; even the kitchen had views of Central Park— one of the many glorious features of this dazzling Park Avenue apartment for the woman who was one of the icons of New York high society.

812 PARK AVENUE

LIVING ROOM
16'-10" X 23'-10"

LIBRARY
16'-6" X 11'-9"

WET BAR

CL

FOYER
15'-0" X 12'-9"

DINING ROOM
17'-8" X 16'-10"

PANTRY

← ENTRY

KITCHEN
13'-4" X 10'-9"

W.I.C.

MAID'S ROOM
12'-0" X 6'-8"

SERVANTS' HALL
9'-6" X 13'-0"

MAID'S ROOM
12'-0" X 8'-0"

CL

CL

MAID'S ROOM
12'-0" X 6'-0"

LOWER LEVEL

MASTER BEDROOM
17'-9" X 16'-0"

DRESSING ROOM
7'-9" X 14'-10"

W.I.C.

CL

CL

CL

CL

CL

W.I.C.

W.I.C.

CL

BEDROOM
20'-0" X 13'-3"

CL

BEDROOM
15'-10" X 12'-10"

UPPER LEVEL

875 PARK AVENUE

885 PARK AVENUE

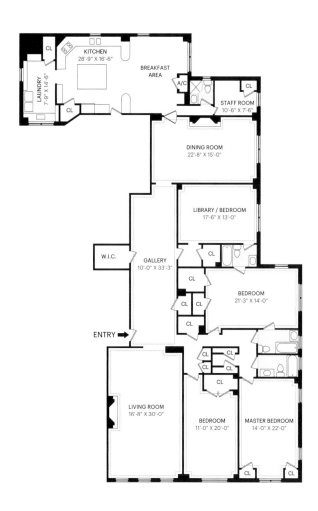

888 PARK AVENUE

940 PARK AVENUE

1040 PARK AVENUE

1088 PARK AVENUE

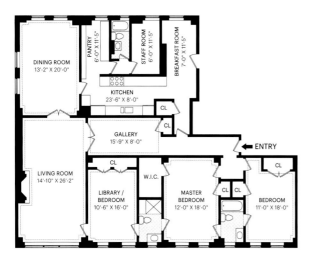

1120 PARK AVENUE

1185 PARK AVENUE

Built on the same massive scale as the Beresford on Central Park West, the 551,000-square-foot 1185 Park Avenue is one of the few remaining prewar courtyard apartment houses, surviving in good company with the Apthorp, the Belnord, and Astor Court on West Eighty-Ninth Street. Others that once existed on Park Avenue south of Fifty-Seventh Street have long since been torn down.

The benefits of these large buildings with enormous floor plates are revealed in the apartments' well-proportioned center-hall plans. Large, family-size classic eights encompass about 3,500 square feet, possessing unexpectedly long entry foyers and exhibiting ideal room relationships. These coveted apartments occupy a niche between the sprawling and stratospherically pricey full-floors with numerous maids' rooms and the much smaller two-bedrooms usually found on the avenue, with enough space for a large family to maintain some privacy. (Another example of a building with family-friendly homes is 173–175 Riverside Drive.)

Though Rosario Candela, Emery Roth, and to some extent J. E. R. Carpenter are the most celebrated prewar architects, it's Schwartz & Gross whose eighteen apartment houses nurtured the calm, consistent, stately red-and-brown-brick architectural tone of Park Avenue. As one heads north toward Ninety-Sixth Street, the firm's work is all around, including addresses 1045, 1070, 1085, 1095, 1111, 1125, and 1165. For 1185 it was hired by the Bricken Construction Company. The developer of 810 Fifth Avenue and 101 Central Park West, Bricken assembled an enormous 201-by-255-foot blockfront between Ninety-Third and Ninety-Fourth Streets, mostly surrounded by low brownstones and walkups, allowing for excellent light and views.

The Venetian Gothic–inspired brick and stone facade of 1185 is similar to that of Schwartz & Gross's 941 Park Avenue, finished fourteen years earlier, and its 888 Park Avenue on the corner of 78th Street—a blend of Gothic, Byzantine, and Moorish influences. On all three buildings, corners are softened by full-height stone spirals, while windows are grouped together in vertical stone bands reminiscent of Venetian palazzos. The three gated Gothic arches distinguish 1185's curbside identity—a grand covered portal opens up to a garden courtyard, like one you might expect at the palace of European royalty.

Inside, its bulk is subdivided into six private lobbies off the courtyard. Throughout fifteen floors there are 165 homes. The 3,800-square-foot A-line classic eights, for example, feature a 27-by-10-foot gallery leading to a 17-by-26-foot living room next to a 14-by-24-foot dining room. There are ten closets and an unusually large kitchen; the master bedroom is on the corner, and each of the three children's bedrooms is generous. Six-room homes maintain similar room proportions, which is rare. The sixteenth-floor penthouse duplex, with 2,500 square feet of terraces on three sides, is reminiscent of a high-floor Candela.

Celebrated novelist Anne Roiphe's *1185 Park Avenue: A Memoir* describes growing up in the building in the 1940s with her family. JPMorgan Chase CEO and chairman Jamie Dimon, one of the few to steer a major bank successfully through the recession of 2008 to 2010, also lives there.

AROUND
THE UPPER
EAST SIDE

TUDOR CITY

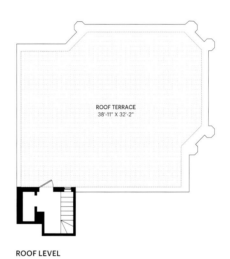

ROOF LEVEL

ROOF TERRACE
38'-11" X 32'-2"

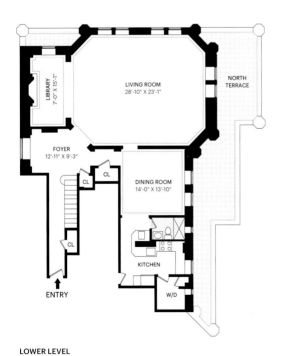

LIBRARY
7'-0" X 15'-1"

LIVING ROOM
28'-10" X 23'-1"

NORTH
TERRACE

FOYER
12'-11" X 9'-3"

CL   CL

DINING ROOM
14'-0" X 13'-10"

CL

KITCHEN

ENTRY

W/D

LOWER LEVEL

OFFICE
7'-8" X 24'-7"

OPEN TO
BELOW

CL   CL

MASTER
BEDROOM
14'-2" X 14'-8"

CL   CL

BEDROOM
14'-1" X 13'-4"

W.I.C.

UPPER LEVEL

435
EAST 52ND
STREET

RIVER HOUSE

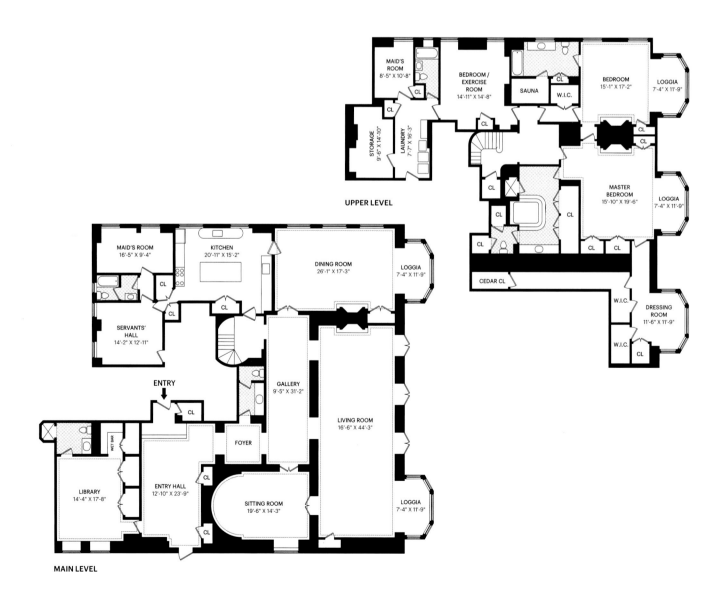

UPPER LEVEL

MAIN LEVEL

Upper Level labels:
MAID'S ROOM 8'-5" X 10'-8"
BEDROOM / EXERCISE ROOM 14'-11" X 14'-8"
SAUNA
W.I.C.
BEDROOM 15'-1" X 17'-2"
LOGGIA 7'-4" X 11'-9"
CL
STORAGE 9'-6" X 14'-10"
LAUNDRY 7'-7" X 16'-3"
MASTER BEDROOM 15'-10" X 19'-6"
LOGGIA 7'-4" X 11'-9"
CEDAR CL
W.I.C.
DRESSING ROOM 11'-6" X 11'-9"

Main Level labels:
MAID'S ROOM 16'-5" X 9'-4"
KITCHEN 20'-11" X 15'-2"
DINING ROOM 26'-1" X 17'-3"
LOGGIA 7'-4" X 11'-9"
SERVANTS' HALL 14'-2" X 12'-11"
ENTRY
GALLERY 9'-5" X 31'-2"
LIVING ROOM 16'-6" X 44'-3"
WET BAR
FOYER
LIBRARY 14'-4" X 17'-8"
ENTRY HALL 12'-10" X 23'-9"
SITTING ROOM 19'-6" X 14'-3"
LOGGIA 7'-4" X 11'-9"

ceilings in the entertaining rooms, which face the river through towering floor-to-ceiling windows; its drawing room alone measures 44 by 16 feet.

The 5,300-square-foot, thirteen-room A-line homes take up the southeast corner of the building. Their public rooms are absolutely majestic in both scale and design. A 30-foot-long entry gallery opens into a living room with three large windows facing the river. The library, through a doorway to the south, has two south-facing windows and a large bay window, also facing the river. The enormous 18 1/2-by-33-foot dining room is on the north side, with its own bay window. Four large bedrooms face south, although there are fewer staff rooms than in earlier apartment houses such as 998 Fifth Avenue.

Little leaks out about the building's residents, though Henry Kissinger, secretary of state under Presidents Richard Nixon and Gerald Ford, is known to be a longtime resident. Blackstone cofounder Peter Peterson, Leeds Equity cofounder Jeffrey Leeds, financier Sir Evelyn de Rothschild, and former Coca-Cola CEO Robert Woodruff had homes there, as did Kiliaen Van Rensselaer, a direct descendant of the founder of the Dutch West India Company, and Cornelius Vanderbilt Whitney, whose mother, Gertrude Vanderbilt Whitney, founded the Whitney Museum of American Art.

Duplex tower units like 22/23, with its sixteen rooms and seven bathrooms, are exceedingly rare in New York. Perhaps only tower homes in the San Remo on Central Park West can compare. The public rooms on the twenty-second floor include a vast 46-by-27-foot drawing room. Upstairs are six large bedrooms, each with spectacular views.

For residents coming home in a chauffeur-driven car, arriving between its tall black gates and pulling up in the circular driveway with a cool breeze off the river, River House has the undeniable presence of an imperial palace. A true masterpiece, the building's remarkable architecture, magnificent homes, and privacy make it inimitably desirable.[9]

Perched on a bluff high above the East River between East Fifty-Second and Fifty-Third Streets, River House is massive. An imposing modernized Georgian masterpiece set behind a tall wrought-iron gate and circular driveway, it is architecturally unlike anything else in the city. A one-off design blending an unusual mix of bay windows and a ziggurat-shaped spire, the building is perfectly composed; it takes several minutes of gazing to absorb the full scope of such a monument. Because high-society prewars are so closely linked to Fifth and Park Avenues, this regal building is an unexpected find at the end of East Fifty-Second Street. Yet that is exactly how residents and its highly selective co-op board prefer it—extremely discreet.

Architecture firm Bottomley, Wagner & White was better known for its movie-ready mansions in Virginia; this apartment house was its only such commission. The site was a rare piece of riverfront property, large enough to accommodate a stand-alone building complete with a private driveway and a dock on the river for residents' yachts.

Taking advantage of the room to spread out, the building is very deliberately not an extruded box. Two fourteen-story wings flank a slender twenty-six-story tower, allowing many homes to have windows on three or even four sides like private homes. Its massing, in fact, steers clear of typical apartment house architecture and has more in common with the designs of art deco skyscrapers like Rockefeller Center or with Hugh Ferriss's iconic black-and-white architectural studies. Only 1 Fifth Avenue, completed five years earlier in 1926, has a similar soft, brown-gray brick, smooth limestone three-story base, and sculpted, tapering form, though it lacks the heavy doses of ornament.

Within its 461,000 square feet are eighty extremely spacious homes. Many of the apartments have seven, eight, or nine rooms; the building also includes a number of duplexes and a still-intact triplex maisonette so large that it has been an albatross for sellers. The triplex boasts 14-foot

14 SUTTON PLACE SOUTH

320 EAST 57TH STREET

136 EAST 64TH STREET

131–135 EAST 66TH STREET

BEDROOM
19'-11" X 14'-0"

OPEN TO BELOW

BEDROOM
14'-8" X 19'-2"

GALLERY

DRESSING ROOM / BEDROOM
9'-9" X 9'-4"

BEDROOM
14'-7" X 10'-6"

CL

UPPER LEVEL

LIBRARY
19'-0" X 16'-0"

LIVING ROOM
24'-0" X 22'-6"

DINING ROOM
19'-9" X 18'-2"

FOYER
8'-2" X 8'-8"

STUDY
9'-2" X 9'-9"

CL

PANTRY
13'-2" X 5'-9"

KITCHEN
19'-0" X 9'-7"

ENTRY

LOWER LEVEL

115 EAST 67TH STREET

MILLAN HOUSE

GARDEN APARTMENT

PENTHOUSE APARTMENT

19 EAST 72ND STREET

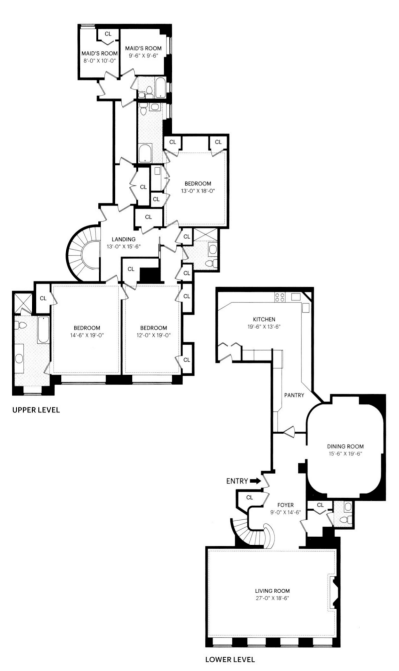

MAID'S ROOM
8'-0" X 10'-0"

MAID'S ROOM
9'-6" X 9'-6"

CL

BEDROOM
13'-0" X 18'-0"

CL CL

CL

LANDING
13'-0" X 15'-6"

CL

CL

CL

BEDROOM
14'-6" X 19'-0"

BEDROOM
12'-0" X 19'-0"

CL

UPPER LEVEL

KITCHEN
19'-6" X 13'-6"

PANTRY

DINING ROOM
15'-6" X 19'-6"

ENTRY ➡

CL

FOYER
9'-0" X 14'-6"

CL

LIVING ROOM
27'-0" X 18'-6"

LOWER LEVEL

In 1934, deep into the Great Depression, General Motors vice president John Thomas Smith bought the immense six-story Romanesque Tiffany mansion on the northwest corner of Seventy-Second Street and Madison Avenue to tear it down. The house looked more like a romantic country hotel than a private home, with a stone base heavy enough to survive a civil war. Five decades earlier, Charles Tiffany had hired a not-yet-thirty-year-old Stanford White to design the house for his growing family, steps from Central Park and the prestigious row of mansions along Fifth Avenue a block away.

Smith hired Rosario Candela to design what would be one of the city's last prewar luxury apartment houses. Candela had recently completed some of the most astonishingly expensive apartment buildings ever constructed, including 740 and 778 Park Avenue just a block away. Architect Mott B. Schmidt was also brought on board to police Candela's

spending. In 1929 Candela's office had opened twelve apartment houses. Between 1931 and September 1937, when 19 East Seventy-Second Street opened, he completed a scant four. New commissions during the Depression were rare, and this would prove to be Candela's last.

Pushing further the art deco and art moderne styles he had explored at 740 Park Avenue, Candela created another limestone iceberg. Almost perfectly flat, it rises straight up from the curb for thirteen floors before stepping back in sharp, clean cuts. The building is topped by outstretched monolithic chimney flues, in keeping with the Egyptian motifs of art deco. Form had replaced ornament as the driver of this building's character, shaping a remarkably powerful architectural statement and a new vision for sheltering the city's elite.

Candela included more duplexes than simplexes, understanding the allure of these spaces with their grand entry foyers. In 1970 high-modern

architect Richard Meier bought and fully renovated a 5,000-square-foot duplex, one of six in the building. If Candela mastered the prewar center-hall floor plan, Meier has arguably invented the modern apartment home. One of the most celebrated architects of our time, he is well known for his pristine, sculpted white spaces. Three of his apartment buildings overlook the Hudson River from the western edge of Greenwich Village, boasting such megawatt residents as domestic diva Martha Stewart, actors Nicole Kidman and Hugh Jackman, and fashion mogul Calvin Klein. Another far larger one commands spectacular views from the edge of Prospect Park in Brooklyn. The floor plans, rooms, and floor-to-ceiling glass walls of Meier's apartments redefine the glamour, grace, and high style of the big-city skyscraper home. Wealthy buyers have flocked to his buildings—the first time that modern apartments have seemed to hold their own against the lure of the prewars.

35 EAST 76TH STREET

1 GRACIE SQUARE

520/530 EAST 86TH STREET

120 EAST END AVENUE

BEDROOM
18'-0" X 15'-5"

MAID'S
ROOM

GYM

DINING ROOM
17'-0" X 16'-0"

CL

CL

CL

KITCHEN

BREAKFAST
ROOM

BEDROOM
14'-0" X 12'-0"

CL

CL

CL

CL

CL

FOYER   ← ENTRY

W.I.C.

CL

MASTER BEDROOM
18'-0" X 18'-5"

LIBRARY LOGGIA
12'-0" X 15'-3"

LIVING ROOM
18'-0" X 23'-8"

UPPER WEST SIDE: CENTRAL PARK WEST

41
CENTRAL
PARK WEST

HARPERLY HALL

55
CENTRAL
PARK WEST

New York's prewar apartment houses are loved for their varying takes on classical architecture. By the late 1920s, architects began experimenting with new ideas of form and ornament, looking more to the future than to styles born in ancient Rome and Renaissance Italy. Minimal ornament and flat walls became fashionable; rather than capping off buildings with heavily decorated horizontal cornice lines, architects placed a new emphasis on the vertical, reaching up and up toward the sky. This was the great age of the steel-frame skyscraper.

The developers of 55 Central Park West, Victor Earle and John C. Calhoun, found this new style of building less costly to produce than older, more ornate models. Completed in 1929, the building is an iconic example of the art deco apartment house. With its modern Gothic spikes in lieu of a cornice and earth-tone brick in gradations from deep purple to limestone white, the apartment house is familiar to many from its starring role in the 1984 film *Ghostbusters*.

Released from classical proportions, 55 Central Park West, with its big, wide windows and sunken living rooms, contains bright spaces that take full advantage of spectacular views of Central Park across the street. A key property of the Central Park West Historic District, it has been home to fashion designers Calvin Klein and Donna Karan; even actress Ginger Rogers lived there while performing on Broadway in the 1930s.

65 CENTRAL PARK WEST

101 CENTRAL PARK WEST

UPPER LEVEL

LOWER LEVEL   *Scale: 1"= 30'– 0"

115 CENTRAL PARK WEST

THE MAJESTIC

The Chanin Construction Company built two twin-tower art deco apartment houses on Central Park West, the Majestic and the Century—both with wide wraparound windows and no columns at the corners. And, like 55 Central Park West farther south, both represented bold architectural moves away from the predominant classical styles, as new expressions of the energy of the late 1920s boom years.

Founded by four brothers—Irwin, Henry, Sam, and Aaron—in Bensonhurst, Brooklyn, the Chanin company rocketed from building small houses to the big time in Manhattan. Although they're best known for the Chanin Building, the fifty-six-story skyscraper across the street from Grand Central Station, they played a far bigger role on Broadway, building six theaters: the 46th Street (now the Richard Rogers), Biltmore (now the Samuel J. Friedman), Mansfield (now the Brooks Atkinson), Theatre Masque (now the John Golden), Royale (now the Bernard B. Jacobs), and Majestic, in addition to the Beacon hotel and theater at Broadway and Seventy-Fifth Street and the gargantuan, now-demolished Roxy movie palace on West Fiftieth Street.[10] The school of architecture at Cooper Union, Irwin Chanin's alma mater, was named after him in 1981.

The Chanins bought and demolished the six-hundred-room Hotel Majestic, across Seventy-Second Street from the Dakota, with plans to build a soaring forty-five-story apartment hotel designed by architecture firm Sloan & Robertson. Stung by the 1929 stock market crash but enabled by the Multiple Dwelling Law, they quickly changed course, reshaping the project into twin towers sitting on a large podium, containing 238 apartment homes and designed in-house by Jacques Delamarre.

Boasting fabulous views of Central Park, most apartments in the Majestic have fireplaces and black walnut floors; some even have sunken living rooms. Although the details are spare and modern, floor plans are classic center-hall.

Late-night talk-show host Conan O'Brien lived in a huge seven-bedroom duplex on the seventeenth and eighteenth floors. Less well known are the building's former Mafia ties. Not only did former heads of the Luciano crime family Lucky Luciano, Frank Costello, and Meyer Lansky make their homes there; in the lobby, in 1957, Costello survived an assassination attempt in the form of a gunshot to the head from Vincent "The Chin" Gigante.

1
WEST 72ND
STREET

THE DAKOTA

When the Dakota's four-year-long construction began in 1880, Central Park was less than a decade old. It's hard to imagine this stretch of Central Park West as mostly unpaved roads, with stray farm animals wandering the streets and shantytowns nearby, but the name "Dakota" seems rather fitting in that context.

The architect was Henry J. Hardenbergh, best known for the Plaza Hotel. He was a pioneer of the still very new apartment house building type that young American architects studying in Europe had brought home. Hardenbergh had been hired by Edward Clark, who had built his fortune as the head of the Singer Sewing Machine Company. The two in many ways invented the luxury Manhattan apartment house. The Dakota boasted rooms of grand proportions and fine woodwork to lure well-off New York families north.

North German Renaissance is the architectural style commonly attached to the Dakota's eclectic mix of fortress-thick walls, steeply pitched roofs, and clusters of very triangular dormers, though the original sixty-five different floor plans were heavily influenced by French apartments of the day. Spacious public rooms, more square in proportion than the narrow rectangles New Yorkers are accustomed to, opened onto one another through large framed doorways. A parallel servant corridor allowed household and kitchen staff to serve the owners and their guests without being seen, as appropriate for an era when wealthy families relied on, and could afford, a large staff.

John Lennon and Yoko Ono, who moved into the Dakota in 1973, brought the building unwanted notoriety. Actors Lauren Bacall, Judy Garland, and Jason Robards; maestro Leonard Bernstein; and dancer Rudolf Nureyev also made their homes in the Dakota. (The building's board is famous for rejecting actors Melanie Griffith and Antonio Banderas.)

Added to the National Register of Historic Places in 1972 and named a National Historic Landmark four years later, the Dakota remains a New York City icon.

145–146 CENTRAL PARK WEST

THE SAN REMO

NORTHEAST TERRACE
13'-6" X 33'-0"

NORTHWEST TERRACE
11'-0" X 16'-0"

SOUTH TERRACE
46'-0" X 19'-0"

STUDY
7'-10" X 10'-2"

KITCHEN
11'-3" X 22'-0"

BREAKFAST ROOM

BALCONY
22'-0" X 4'-0"

DN

DINING ROOM
13'-8" X 17'-7"

LIVING ROOM
21'-8" X 21'-4"

W.I.C.   W.I.C.

ENTRY

GALLERY / LIBRARY
17'-0" X 11'-9"

ELEV

BEDROOM
11'-6" X 13'-6"

BEDROOM
11'-6" X 9'-0"

CL

W.I.C.

MASTER BEDROOM
20'-2" X 17'-7"

The San Remo is one of New York's architectural trophies. Conceived during the Roaring Twenties' extraordinary building boom, it was constructed as the city was swiftly establishing itself as an international business center and fertile ground for great architecture. Architect Emery Roth took advantage of the new Multiple Dwelling Law to refine the ideas of the skyscraper home he had developed at the Ritz on Park Avenue and sculpt a twenty-seven-story, twin-tower urban masterpiece.

Yet glamour quickly fades, and in 1940, as New York's and the rest of the country's economy groaned under the financial weight of supporting the Allies during World War II, both the

San Remo and the Beresford (a short walk up Central Park West at Eighty-First Street) were sold for a mere $25,000 over their mortgages, eventually regaining their footing as co-ops in the 1970s.

On a typical floor in the San Remo's podium, three apartments face the park, and two on each side face Seventy-Fourth and Seventy-Fifth Streets. C-line apartments in the southeast corner, some of the finest and most spacious Roth designed, are 4,500-square-foot classic eights. Ceilings are an impressive 11 feet. Living rooms are 600 square feet, the size of a typical one-bedroom apartment, and details are exquisite and understated.

But it's the coveted full-floor tower apartments, rare in their privacy, views, and natural light, that have attracted A-list residents such as director Steven Spielberg; Apple cofounder Steve Jobs; rock star Bono; and actors Rita Hayworth, Glenn Close, and Demi Moore. Moore's penthouse triplex in the south tower is almost 7,000 square feet and one of the largest homes on Central Park West.

The building's postcard elegance—part monument, part palace, and perfectly proportioned—encapsulates why prewars are so desirable. Standing in Central Park, admiring it from across the boat pond, who wouldn't dream of living there someday?

211 CENTRAL PARK WEST

THE BERESFORD

It's hard not to be captivated by the colossal Beresford. With twenty-three floors overlooking both Central Park and the grounds of the American Museum of Natural History, it was among the largest and grandest luxury apartment houses ever built when it was completed in 1929. A New York City landmark easily recognizable by its three corner cupolas, it has the air of a Jazz Age castle. As an architectural masterpiece, it's a monument to New York's ambition to be the greatest city on earth.

The building was named after the Hotel Beresford, which occupied the site from 1889 until 1927. Developed by HRH Construction, the Beresford has a U-shaped plan that takes advantage of a rare 200-by-200-foot property large enough to allow

for a three-sided courtyard. There are three separate entrances and elevator cores, making a very large building far more private than you'd expect—many apartments have their own elevator vestibule.

Homes inside are Emery Roth classics with sprawling center-hall plans, dotted with terraces of varying shapes and sizes as the building tapers skyward. The immense footprint of the building, like those of other courtyard buildings such as the Apthorp or 1185 Park Avenue, allows for remarkable room dimensions and enormous entry galleries. Rare for a prewar, particularly one of 600,000 square feet, the homes are bright, with many living rooms having three windows side-by-side instead of just two and spectacular views, particularly from the upper floors.

Unlike many other co-ops wary of public figures who might attract unwanted media attention, it has been open to politicians and celebrities. Current and former residents include singer Diana Ross; operatic soprano Beverly Sills; foreign-policy czar Richard Holbrooke; and actors Jerry Seinfeld, Glenn Close, Tony Randall, Rock Hudson, and Andrew McCarthy.

Under each of the three cupolas is an almighty four-story penthouse primed for the kings of New York; tennis great John McEnroe and Miramax cofounder Bob Weinstein are former owners. Topped by soaring lounges in the cupolas with dramatic arched windows and featuring three exposures, these three homes rarely come on the market. They are part of why the Beresford is one of the most dramatic addresses in New York.

300 CENTRAL PARK WEST

THE ELDORADO

Despite the completion of the Dakota in 1884, Central Park West, unlike Fifth Avenue, didn't really start becoming the wall of luxury apartment houses we see today until the late 1920s.

The thirty-story Eldorado, developed by Louis Klosk from the Bronx, is the northernmost of the four twin-tower apartment houses on Central Park West. Built between 1929 and 1931, it fills out the blockfront between Ninetieth and Ninety-First Streets and looks out over Central Park's Jacqueline Kennedy Onassis Reservoir, a small lake circled by a well-worn dirt jogging path. Architect Margon & Holder (with Emery Roth as an adviser) designed a striking tapered, futuristic design in the art deco style, exhibiting remarkable restraint as well as architectural resolution.

Details throughout are daring and beautiful. A strong emphasis on the vertical, like at 55 Central Park West, leads to the twin spires with what Elliot Willensky in *The AIA Guide to New York City* calls "Flash Gordon finials."[11]

Past the lobby, the 216 apartment homes stick more closely to the feel and details of classic center-hall prewars, yet are smaller than some of the huge apartments down the street. For example, in 8A, the entry gallery is an art-collection-ready 7 1/2 by 29 1/2 feet, and the living room is 16 by 28 feet. At the top of the south tower, there's a spectacular four-story penthouse once owned by the musician Moby. Each floor has essentially one room with unobstructed views in four directions, and a handful of terraces to boot.

Barney Pressman, who founded the much-admired Barneys department store, purchased a home in the Eldorado

just as it opened. Other residents have included actors Alec Baldwin, Faye Dunaway, Groucho Marx, and Marilyn Monroe. The building became a co-op in 1982 and was designated a New York City landmark in 1985.[12]

UPPER WEST SIDE: WEST END AVENUE

300 WEST END AVENUE

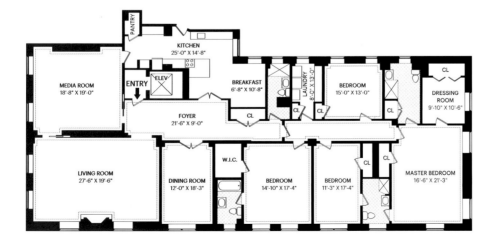

450 WEST END AVENUE

BEDROOM
14'-0" X 19'-0"

LIVING ROOM
16'-0" X 27'-0"

CL CL

CL

CL

ENTRY →

GALLERY
11'-0" X 11'-0"

CL

BEDROOM
19'-0" X 12'-0"

W.I.C.

KITCHEN
8'-2" X 17'-0"

MAID'S ROOM
7'-1" X 12'-0"

DINING ROOM
20'-0" X 14'-0"

BALCONY

530 WEST END AVENUE

THE SEXTON

Architects Harry Mulliken and Edgar Moeller both graduated from the Columbia University School of Architecture in 1895. They had begun their practice together by 1902 and got their start designing hotels in the Upper West Side for James and David Todd (whose family firm was later renamed the Todd, Robertson, Todd Engineering Corporation and would go on to build two city landmarks: Rockefeller Center and the Cunard Building at 25 Broadway). Mulliken & Moeller's Bretton Hall Hotel, minus its cornice, is still standing just a block east of the Sexton on Broadway between Eighty-Fifth and Eighty-Sixth Streets.

In 1905 the Todds launched Mulliken & Moeller into the world of apartment houses with commissions for the Severn and the Van Dyck, both on Amsterdam Avenue. These were followed by the design for a different developer of a pair of twelve-story apartment houses on Central Park West, numbers 251 and 257. For these early projects, Mulliken & Moeller experimented with and developed its architectural trademark, "a vigorous contrast of flat brick and extensive, highly sculptured cream-colored terra cotta, often organized around a large central bay."[13] The firm was also known for a bold use of form and color (at times resulting in buildings that were a bit gaudy, but that had a strong identity on the street—particularly important for hotels).

By 1912, for the thirteen-story 530 West End Avenue, they took a dramatic turn away from vivid, contrasting colors. On the southeast corner of Eighty-Sixth Street and West End Avenue, the tone-on-tone composition, like a giant sand castle, relies only on light and shadow to bring out the shapes of its Spanish Baroque terra-cotta facade. The Sexton is reminiscent of the refined limestone structures of Fifth Avenue or the nearby Apthorp and Belnord, finished a few years earlier. Far less aggressive than Mulliken & Moeller's previous designs—and perhaps its finest work—the Sexton's facade displayed a restraint in keeping with the luxury apartments inside. Some were as large as seventeen rooms, with 11-foot ceilings and only two homes per floor. There are fireplaces in not just the living rooms but the dining rooms and master bedrooms, too.

The building's forty-five apartments are fortunate to have survived the Upper West Side's decline in the 1970s and 1980s, when many large prewar homes were chopped up into small rental units. Featuring grand rooms and tasteful details, the Sexton continues to provide hard-to-find family-size homes.

800 WEST END AVENUE

Rosario Candela is best known for his high-wattage co-ops on the Upper East Side. For those in the know, his finest buildings, such as 740 and 778 Park Avenue and 834 Fifth Avenue, are often referred to by only their street number—740, 778, or 834. However, Candela applied what he learned from apartment homes that pushed the extremes of urban luxury to the many more-modest apartment houses he designed, including eight on West End Avenue—in particular, number 800.

Gracious, sprawling center-hall plans reflect Candela's fine hand. The F-line apartments are 1,800-square-foot two-bedroom homes, with entry foyers reaching 27 feet long. The living rooms alone are 14 feet wide and 25 feet long, situated far from the front door for privacy.

Its sand-colored brick Renaissance Revival facade doesn't boast cascading terraces, as some of his taller buildings do; nor do the five other Candelas within a few blocks of number 800, and unfortunately, a few of their cornices have been removed. Yet 800's proud and understated architecture conceals some of Candela's hidden gems in the neighborhood.

UPPER WEST SIDE: RIVERSIDE DRIVE

33 RIVERSIDE DRIVE

90 RIVERSIDE DRIVE

140 RIVERSIDE DRIVE

THE NORMANDY

On a bluff towering over the Hudson River at the west end of Eighty-Sixth Street, the twin spires and smooth, curved art moderne corners of the Normandy mark the end of New York's great era of prewar apartment houses. In stark contrast to the late 1920s, when Manhattan must have seemed like one big construction site, luxury apartment house construction had all but vanished during the economic abyss of the 1930s.

When the Normandy was completed in 1940, a sixty-nine-year-old Emery Roth was trying to slow down. After a very lean decade, he had passed on the day-to-day running of his firm to his son Richard. The company, renamed Emery Roth & Sons in 1947, would go on to thrive in the postwar boom of glass-walled-office-building construction, as all but one of the luxury apartment houses within prime walking distance of Grand Central on Park Avenue south of Fifty-Seventh Street met the wrecking ball. The demolished included two striking courtyard examples: Warren & Wetmore's two-block-long 270 Park Avenue, named the Mansions, and McKim, Mead & White's 277.

With twenty stories enclosing 372,000 square feet, the Normandy was a massive, more up-to-date version of the Beresford and the San Remo, displaying a sleek, streamlined modern glamour. Its design was inspired by the largest and fastest ocean liner of the day, the French SS *Normandie*, which on its maiden voyage in June 1935 from Le Havre to New York had shattered the transatlantic speed record. The metaphor of the ocean liner determined the building's curved corners, strong horizontal lines cutting through a limestone base, and wide windows overlooking the river. A glassy loggia connects the two circular street lobbies on Eighty-Sixth and Eighty-Seventh Streets, overlooking a sunken garden. With the Normandy and also with 875 Fifth Avenue, finished the year before, Roth's son was pulling away from the rigid classical forms that had been the backbone of prewar architecture.

Room sizes were still generous by today's standards, offering 13-by-24-foot living rooms next to 12-by-20-foot bedrooms. Dining rooms were often shrunk to cute semicircular dinettes,

while minidorms of maids' rooms disappeared altogether. Wood-burning fireplaces were few, yet hard-to-resist herringbone wood floors were standard features. Late 1920s–style sprawling eight-, nine-, and ten-room homes made way for big one- and two-bedrooms. Families had fallen hard for the proud houses, clean air, and car-oriented lifestyle of the leafy suburbs around the city, making classic sevens and eights harder to sell.

N-, P-, and M-line one-bedrooms are huge, and E-line studios are lovely. Today it's hard to imagine entering a studio through an 8-by-12-foot foyer, into a 13-by-24-foot living room with a separate curved sleeping alcove boasting river views. There's a dressing room and three closets, too. Prime corner views were reserved for A-line classic sixes and K-line classic sevens, with center-hall plans straight out of Roth's more conventional playbook. Commanding extraordinary views from wraparound terraces, the penthouses rise above almost everything in the surrounding neighborhood, affording precious moments of solitude amid the bustle of the city.

173–175 RIVERSIDE DRIVE

was completed in 1913, as he launched his architectural career. Although many were later subdivided, there originally were only two enormous apartments per floor, with either twelve or fourteen rooms and four baths. Its plan and elevation were very similar to those of 960 Park Avenue, which he had completed a year earlier.

The fifteen-story 173–175 Riverside Drive, the finest address on the street and a Gothic-inspired masterpiece of apartment house design, was commissioned by prominent developer Anthony Campagna, also Carpenter's client at 960 Park Avenue. Its odd-shaped, curving lot faces the Hudson River and the Soldiers' and Sailors' Monument, which commemorates the Union troops who served in the American Civil War.

The building contains a striking mix of 167 elegant homes. It is really two separate addresses, with entrances on both Eighty-Ninth and Ninetieth Streets. To ensure privacy, each address is further divided into two elevator cores, which for the most part give access to only two apartments per floor. L-line one-bedrooms have an extraordinary 20-foot-long entrance gallery, a 22-by-13-foot living room, a fireplace, and a separate 13-by-17-foot dining room. B-line duplexes, such as 10/11B and 12/13B, boast 3,000 square feet of living space, each with a library and south-facing views.

Yet the floor-through, nine-room D-lines are most sought after, with their well-proportioned center-hall plans. The entrance is through a 29-foot-long gallery leading to a combined 45-foot-long living and dining room, with windows facing both west toward the Hudson and east toward Central Park. Each bedroom also has a river view.

The chamfered southwest corner facing the river contains the C-line unit. Center-hall plans struggle against this angle in order to keep rooms strict rectangles, so that much of the acute angle of the building corner isn't noticeable, except in one corridor. But contained in the chamfer, bathed in afternoon light, is a good-sized child's bedroom with an astonishing view.

J. E. R. Carpenter, more than any other prewar-era architect, mastered the art of refined restraint. His facades sometimes seem almost flat, free of ornament or even a cornice except for a few thin stone bands, revealing his exceedingly fine attention to detail and minimal approach to classical architectural forms. The Upper East Side was his canvas; he designed a remarkable eighteen apartment houses on Fifth Avenue facing Central Park and another thirteen on Park Avenue, wielding enormous influence on the architectural tone of the two streets.

Carpenter designed only two apartment houses on the other side of the park. Howard House stands on the northeast corner of Seventy-First Street, at 246 West End Avenue, and

258 RIVERSIDE DRIVE
THE PETER STUYVESANT

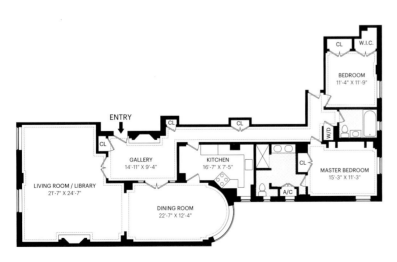

Walking up Riverside Drive as it gently curves toward the river, you can't miss the building on the corner of Ninety-Eighth Street: the three-story-tall diamond brick pattern, interrupted by immense arched windows outlined in deep blue terra-cotta, provides a brilliant pop of color in a city of grit-covered reds, browns, beiges, and black. At the third-floor level is another band of arched windows. The massive entryway is worthy of Rome, protected by a heavy, black gate of tightly knit wrought iron.

The building was completed in 1912 for two budding developers, James T. Lee (who would later build 740 Park Avenue) and Charles Fleischmann. Topping out at thirteen floors, it's named after Peter Stuyvesant, the last director general of New Amsterdam from 1647 until 1664, when it was handed over to the British and became New York. Perhaps the front gate of 258 Riverside is so robust to remind us of the outsized legacy of the man who built the wall at Wall Street.

Long since gone are the building's massive cornice, which once hung out over the sidewalk, and its lovely offset balconies. Yet inside the building, 10-foot ceilings, the marble street lobby, and mosaic tile floors at the elevator landings are much the same as when they were designed by the building's architect, William L. Rouse. Of the fifty-one homes, most were originally drafted with separate libraries. The two-bedroom B-lines wrap the northwest corner, with three big windows facing the Hudson River, while the D-line apartments also face the river and have lovely beamed-ceiling dining rooms, each with a curved wall of windows facing south.

Rouse first established himself by designing the romantic Tuscan-themed apartment house up the street, 380 Riverside Drive, for developers George F. Johnson Jr. and Aleck Kahn. That building is elaborately done up, with two bell towers connected by a loggia and Spanish tile roofs hanging well over the sidewalk. Later, as part of Rouse & Goldstone, he would design almost twenty more apartment houses, but his architecture would take a radical turn in personality. It's hard to believe that the muted brick tones of 755 Park Avenue, enclosing absolutely huge center-hall apartment mansions, came from the same hand. Numbers 270 and 276 Riverside Drive would display a similar sense of calm. By 1925 Rouse's career topper would be 1107 Fifth Avenue, home to the fifty-four-room triplex penthouse he designed for Marjorie Merriweather Post Hutton, who with her husband founded General Foods. On a colossal scale matching Mar-a-Lago, the home Joseph Urban designed for Hutton in Palm Beach, it was at that time the largest apartment in the city, essentially recreating the townhouse she had previously owned on the site.

310 RIVERSIDE DRIVE

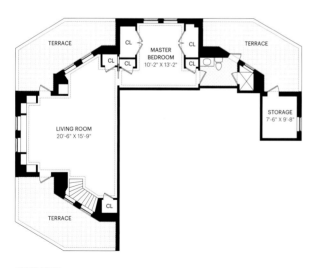

TERRACE

CL   MASTER BEDROOM
10'-2" X 13'-2"   CL

TERRACE

CL   CL   CL

LIVING ROOM
20'-6" X 15'-9"

STORAGE
7'-6" X 9'-8"

CL

TERRACE

UPPER LEVEL

ENTRY

KITCHEN / DINING
15'-0" X 17'-5"   FOYER
7'-10" X 11'-2"   BEDROOM
11'-4" X 11'-2"   CL

CL

LOWER LEVEL

315 RIVERSIDE DRIVE

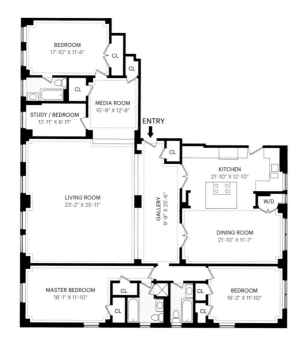

BEDROOM
17'-10" X 11'-6"

CL

CL

CL

MEDIA ROOM
10'-9" X 12'-8"

STUDY / BEDROOM
12'-11" X 6'-11"

ENTRY

CL

KITCHEN
21'-10" X 12'-10"

LIVING ROOM
23'-2" X 25'-11"

GALLERY
9'-9" X 25'-6"

W/D

DINING ROOM
21'-10" X 11'-7"

MASTER BEDROOM
18'-1" X 11'-10"

CL

CL

CL

CL

BEDROOM
16'-2" X 11'-10"

440 RIVERSIDE DRIVE

THE PATERNO

Riverside Drive's curves and grassy, rolling hills are reminiscent of a sleepy country lane next to Manhattan's rigid street grid and tall buildings. But it's only a short block from its eastern neighbor, West End Avenue, which, in contrast, is loaded up with an astonishing ten million square feet of apartments as it runs dead straight for almost forty blocks. In Morningside Heights, a magnificent curved gateway guides pedestrians from Riverside Park up 116th Street to the gates of Columbia University. Nearby, two giant, curved brick facades face each other on a scale you'd expect on a grand avenue in Paris, not in make-it-straight New York.

Both buildings were designed by prolific architecture firm Schwartz & Gross. The much larger and more imposing 440 Riverside Drive is on the north side of the street; the smaller number 435, originally consisting

of full-floor homes, is on the south side. Like the Dakota when it was completed way uptown on a very bare Central Park West in 1884, these two buildings needed to be showstoppers. The building's young developer, the Paterno Construction Company, commissioned striking architecture to lure renters to this large apartment house so far from the offices downtown.

Completed in 1909, five years after the 116th Street subway stop a block away, the architecture is typical of early apartment houses: grand, showy, and heavily ornamented, it's almost hard to distinguish from an important civic building. The romantic triple-arched porte cochere of 440 allowed a resident's horse and carriage to pull in out of the rain. The vast marble lobby inside is well known for its stunning stained-glass ceiling. This building is a superb example of how more-modest

apartment houses maintained the richness and urban glamour of those on Fifth and Park Avenues—in this case, with spectacular views and a location steps from one of the best parts of Riverside Park.

Three-bedroom apartments in the building's southwest corner have the best floor plans. Each has a small foyer; the parlor, dining, and living rooms are aligned in a row and open to one another, separated only by arched openings with lovely French doors. In the corner facing south toward the Hudson River is one of the best master bedrooms in the city. Even the smaller apartments of 440 are charmers, with their tall baseboards, wood paneling, chandeliers, and imposing fireplaces. It's easy to understand why location scouts proposed 440 Riverside as a setting for the Disney movie *Enchanted*, about a fairy-tale princess who finds herself in New York City.

AROUND
THE UPPER
WEST SIDE

1
WEST 67TH STREET

HOTEL DES ARTISTES

UPPER LEVEL

LOWER LEVEL

2109 BROADWAY
THE ANSONIA

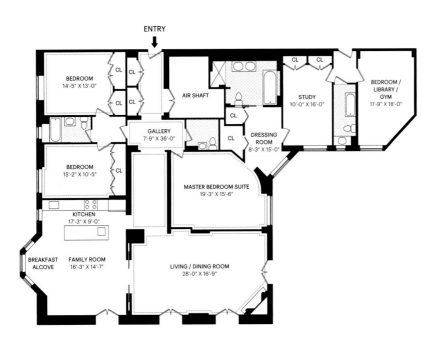

ENTRY

BEDROOM
14'-5" X 13'-0"

CL CL

CL CL

CL CL

AIR SHAFT

CL CL

STUDY
10'-0" X 16'-0"

BEDROOM /
LIBRARY /
GYM
11'-9" X 18'-0"

CL

GALLERY
7'-9" X 36'-0"

CL

DRESSING
ROOM
8'-3" X 15'-0"

BEDROOM
15'-2" X 10'-5"

CL

MASTER BEDROOM SUITE
19'-3" X 15'-6"

KITCHEN
17'-3" X 9'-0"

BREAKFAST
ALCOVE

FAMILY ROOM
16'-3" X 14'-7"

LIVING / DINING ROOM
28'-0" X 16'-9"

When it opened on April 19, 1904, the Ansonia was designed to be the most luxurious residential hotel in New York. It could handle an astonishing thirteen hundred dinner guests at a time, and it was the first apartment building to have air conditioning, through a system of steel flues that circulated freezing brine. The world's largest indoor pool at the time was in the basement, and live seals frolicked in the lobby fountain.

The copper heir William Earle Dodges Stokes, born in 1852, was a prominent advocate and row house developer of the Upper West Side. Though he took the title of "architect in chief" for the Ansonia, he hired architect and sculptor Paul E. M. Duboy to design the building. From the photo-op view outside the Seventy-Second Street subway station, the eighteen-floor Ansonia—at a hefty 550,000 square feet—seems even larger. The very romantic and very French Beaux-Arts architecture is no doubt grand, and its gorgeous, winding, skylit, marble open stair is a must-see for any New Yorker. Stokes even developed a rooftop farm when the hotel opened, stocked with chickens, ducks, goats, and at times cattle, brought up by a dedicated cattle elevator.

Though the current 390 apartments predate the age of the center-hall plan, rooms have up to 12-foot ceilings and enormous windows extending almost to the floor. Those rooms facing the street are remarkably bright for a prewar; most desirable of all are the apartments with a living room in the circular turret.

The Ansonia was Babe Ruth's first home in New York, after he was sold to the Yankees by the Boston Red Sox. In the late 1970s and early 1980s, the building was infamous for housing the popular swingers' club Plato's Retreat in the basement. Designated a New York City landmark in 1972 and added to the National Register of Historic Places in 1980, it also played roles in the films *Single White Female* and Neil Simon's *The Sunshine Boys*.[14]

161 WEST 75TH STREET

OFFICE / BEDROOM
15'-0" X 7'-3"

LAUNDRY
10'-0" X 6'-9"

W.I.C.

CL

BEDROOM
13'-6" X 9'-6"

DRESSING ROOM
18'-0" X 7'-6"

W/D

CL

MASTER BEDROOM
14'-0" X 21'-0"

W.I.C.

BEDROOM
12'-10" X 16'-8"

UPPER LEVEL

MAID'S ROOM
11'-7" X 7'-0"

ENTRY

KITCHEN
16'-9" X 20'-0"

FOYER
15'-8" X 6'-4"

CL

CL

CL

CL

LIVING ROOM
16'-0" X 22'-6"

DINING ROOM
13'-0" X 22'-6"

CL

BEDROOM
12'-0" X 16'-6"

LOWER LEVEL

6-16 WEST 77TH STREET

UPPER LEVEL

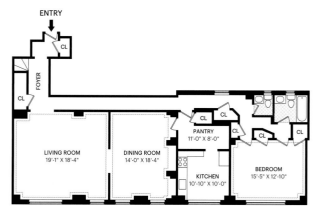

LOWER LEVEL

2211 BROADWAY

THE APTHORP

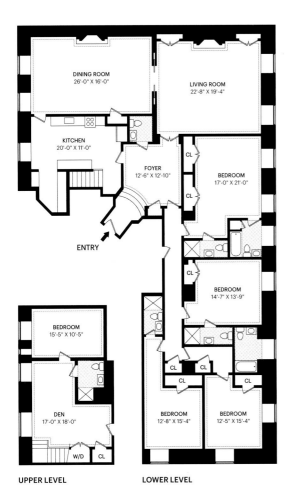

DINING ROOM
26'-0" X 16'-0"

LIVING ROOM
22'-8" X 19'-4"

KITCHEN
20'-0" X 11'-0"

FOYER
12'-6" X 12'-10"

CL

BEDROOM
17'-0" X 21'-0"

CL

ENTRY

BEDROOM
14'-7" X 13'-9"

CL

BEDROOM
15'-5" X 10'-5"

DEN
17'-0" X 18'-0"

CL CL

CL

CL

BEDROOM
12'-8" X 15'-4"

BEDROOM
12'-5" X 15'-4"

W/D CL

UPPER LEVEL   **LOWER LEVEL**

It is a building coveted like few others, with a noble name that perfectly suits the architecture. Without question, the Apthorp is one of the finest and most inspiring examples of Italian Renaissance Revival architecture in New York, drawing its proportions and imperial weight from the Pitti Palace in Florence. If it's possible to have a love affair with an apartment house, it's what screenwriter Nora Ephron described in a 2006 piece for the *New Yorker* about her ten years living in a fifth-floor, eight-room home for a scandalous $1,500 a month.[15]

In the early eighteenth century, before there was the Upper West Side, Charles Ward Apthorp (the eldest of the eighteen children of Charles Apthorp, at one time said to be the richest man in Boston) owned a 300-acre parcel named Apthorp Farm. Located roughly between West Eighty-Ninth and Ninety-Ninth Streets, it spanned from Central Park all the way to the Hudson River. Though hard to believe, legal fighting between the family heirs prevented speculative development of this land until 1910.

A small mountain of luxury, the Apthorp was developed by William Waldorf Astor, who in 1890 became the richest man in America overnight when he inherited his father's fur

and real estate fortune. By 1893 he had already completed construction of what was then the world's most luxurious hotel, designed by Henry J. Hardenbergh, the 450-room Waldorf on the corner of Thirty-Third Street and Fifth Avenue—the hub for the city's fashionable society. (As high society progressively moved farther uptown, riding the wave of the city's growth up Fifth Avenue, it was demolished in 1929 to make way for the Empire State Building.)

The architecture of the Apthorp, built between 1906 and 1908, tempted future residents with the royal scale of a European palace. Surrounded by a narrow, waterless moat, it stands alone, consuming an entire city block on the southwest corner of Seventy-Ninth Street and Broadway. The facade—not just the base—is fully clad in massive limestone blocks. At its crown is a deep, very green copper-clad cornice, heavily ornamented and reaching far out over the sidewalk below. Though its bare, sheer stone walls appear cold, they are meant to be impressive; palaces aren't friendly.

Inside, the Apthorp boasts manned elevators (each with a chandelier and a bench), soaring ceilings, marble fireplaces, and four private lobbies, each leading to just three homes per

floor. The center-hall apartment plans have graciously proportioned rooms. Actor Al Pacino, late-night host Conan O'Brien, pop star Cyndi Lauper, and television personality Rosie O'Donnell have lived there.

It's the Apthorp's glorious limestone-clad courtyard that truly inspires the public's imagination. From outside the wrought-iron bars of the gate, through the dim, vaulted gateway, entranced passersby can catch a peek of the world of privilege inside. A circular driveway wraps around a garden with two gurgling fountains, allowing cars to drop residents off at each of the four lobbies. At 95 feet wide by 130 feet long, it's one of the biggest private outdoor spaces in the city.

Some homes face the street, some face the courtyard, and some span the width of the building to face both. Many early apartment houses drew complaints that apartments on the back were dreary and dark, with some looking straight into brick walls. But the Apthorp's courtyard, with its facade just like the one facing the street, means there's in effect no backside; courtyard views are even better than street views, and far quieter. The Apthorp's courtyard is perhaps New York City's most amazing front door.

15 WEST 81ST STREET

Emery Roth's genius was his ability to design fine architecture within the very limited means available to most Manhattan residential real estate speculators. Brick facades had to go straight up from the sidewalk to maximize floor space. Details were few to keep costs down. And ideally, only one window size was used, repeated hundreds of times to keep construction simple, fast, and cheap. In response, Roth's work reveals an intense focus on window proportion and rhythm, while humanizing the scale of these big buildings with small areas of intense detail around windows and doors. (Roth's skill was shared by Rosario Candela and, particularly, by J. E. R. Carpenter.)

The American Museum of Natural History opened in 1877, amid small farms and brand-new city grid streets, yet few buildings. A wave of row house construction rolling north had reached this stretch of West Eighty-First Street by the 1880s. By 1930 all but 33 West Eighty-First Street were gone, replaced by huge new apartment houses.

With views straight south, at and mostly over the museum, the sixteen-story 15 West Eighty-First Street is an impressive example of tough-to-design midblock architecture. Usually, developers assembled 100-by-100-foot corner lots. In spite of its bulk (about 325,000 square feet, with 119 apartments), the fine neo-Renaissance details, used very sparingly, give it an intimacy and a well-dressed fine grain. The massive water-tower enclosure on top, disguised as a bell tower, is a familiar Emery Roth move, using historical architectural components borrowed from civic buildings to add drama to what are otherwise flat, uneventful cornice lines.

The apartments, mostly two-bedrooms, are characteristic Roth. Living rooms—like those at his famous Beresford down the street, built at the same time—are centered on large windows, many offering views of the museum. Some are as large as 25 by 18 feet, with prominent fireplaces. Each is entered through a wide vestibule and possesses a spaciousness and natural light not often seen in older prewars.

Roth's genius is readily apparent in the way he shaped these marvelous urban homes, along with the skill he put into the many small design decisions that make fine residential architecture. These family-friendly apartment homes can affect the health and vitality of an entire metropolis like New York; imagine how lifeless the city would be if everyone with children commuted from the suburbs instead of living in Manhattan.

221 WEST 82ND STREET

200 WEST 86TH STREET

THE NEW AMSTERDAM

TERRACE

BEDROOM
16'-10" X 15'-7"

W.I.C.

W.I.C.

W.I.C.

BEDROOM
11'-9" X 20'-11"

W.I.C. CL

DINING ROOM
13'-9" X 17'-9"

ENTRY CL

LIVING ROOM
25'-9" X 12'-10"

GALLERY
14'-7" X 7'-8"

KITCHEN
7'-6" X 14'-0"

CL

TERRACE

BEDROOM
17'-8" X 13'-9"

225
WEST 86TH
STREET
THE BELNORD

Eight blocks farther north on Broadway than the Apthorp and opened one year later, another colossal courtyard apartment house was completed by William Waldorf Astor. The Belnord, 50 percent larger than the Apthorp, was at the time the biggest apartment building in the world, enclosing an extraordinary 665,000 square feet and covering an entire city block to rise straight up thirteen floors—a whale of a building, compared with the minnowlike town houses that lined the side streets around it.

In the first decade of the twentieth century, ever-taller steel-frame buildings were being constructed quickly throughout the city at an unimaginable scale, transforming streetscapes in ways the world had never seen. Astor hired the society architects of Hiss & Weekes to design the Belnord. Though untested in the building type—and certainly at such an extreme scale—Hiss & Weekes clearly understood how the well-off wanted to live. The firm had recently completed the luxurious Gotham Hotel (now the Peninsula) in 1905, across

Fifth Avenue from the St. Regis. More important was their growing portfolio of magnificent country estates on Long Island's Gold Coast and Southampton, which would eventually include the well-known Hoyt, Westerly, and Baker residences. Oddly, the exiled King Zog of Albania bought their sprawling Knollwood estate in 1951 in Muttontown, New York, yet never moved in.

For more than a hundred years, the Belnord has been a private world, centered on its enormous 231-by-94-foot landscaped courtyard. When built, it offered the latest in modern conveniences: refrigerators that made ice, central vacuum systems, a gated private driveway inside the courtyard for carriages, and even a subterranean truck court entered down a ramp off Eighty-Seventh Street to conceal from residents the sight of trash and deliveries.

Like the Apthorp's, the Belnord's center-hall plans were remarkably well resolved as the basis of graceful homes that steered clear of the problems plaguing many early

prewars—dark air shafts and no view from apartments at the back. Its eight- to fourteen-room homes vary in size and configuration to appeal to different families' needs. Some have libraries and as many as twelve closets, in addition to herringbone wood floors and fireplaces (often in both living and dining rooms); each has a large foyer entered from a semiprivate elevator landing. Bedrooms, many with bay windows, generally face the courtyard, where there's no street noise.

Centered on the building's west side (facing Broadway), matching the width of the courtyard, is a sprawling classic eight with a 15-by-26-foot entry gallery, ideal for entertaining (the parlor and dining room are actually smaller). On the northeast and southeast corners are classic sevens similar to compact town houses, where almost all the rooms are the same size. On the east side (facing Amsterdam Avenue) are two mirrored classic sixes where the dining room, parlor, and living room are side by side, creating a vast room with two fireplaces spanning from street to courtyard. For privacy, there are six separate passenger-elevator cores, paired with eight service-elevator cores.

A designated New York City landmark since 1966, the massive Belnord was added to the National Register of Historic Places in 1980. This Renaissance Revival building may be huge, yet it surprisingly seems to fit in seamlessly on the Upper West Side. Small shopfronts cut into the massive walls reduce its bulk, as does the heavy banding in the building's limestone base. The Belnord's most glorious feature is the pair of side-by-side vaulted archways in the middle of the Eighty-Sixth Street facade. Roman-inspired red frescoes are visible on their curved ceiling from outside the gated and guarded entranceway; the greenery and calm of the courtyard inside are enhanced by clusters of illuminated globes.[16] The Belnord continues to offer its residents grand gestures and marvelous common spaces that few, no matter how rich, could afford themselves.

DOWNTOWN

1 FIFTH AVENUE

Surrounding Washington Square Park is a neighborhood chock-full of darling three- and four-story town houses next to boxy New York University buildings. None is too remarkable on its own, but together the narrow streets and varying warm brick tones make for some of the best strolling anywhere.

Few towers have such an iconic location as 1 Fifth Avenue. A twenty-seven-story lightning rod, reaching high above almost everything around, it's in the background of almost every tourist photo of the square's central fountain and grand white marble arch (which a decade ago received a long-overdue scrubbing and new lighting). Like many beloved monuments, its reason for being has been all but forgotten, but the arch at the foot of Fifth Avenue was built in 1892 to commemorate the centennial of President George Washington's inauguration and was designed by Stanford White.

Architects Sugarman & Berger teamed up with Helmle, Corbett & Harrison. The former had designed the hulking, tapered New Yorker Hotel at Eighth Avenue and Thirty-Fourth Street, as well as a few more-sedate apartment houses such as 239 and 262 Central Park West. Wallace K. Harrison, of Helmle, Corbett & Harrison, later became known for very large-scale city projects as a key player in the design of the United Nations headquarters, Rockefeller Center, and the master plan for Lincoln Center. Helmle, Corbett & Harrison also later designed what was supposed to be the tallest skyscraper in the world, at 11 Madison Avenue, but construction stopped at the twenty-ninth floor in 1933.

Because 1 Fifth was developed by Joseph G. Siegel as an apartment hotel with food service, it has small apartments and even smaller kitchens. The exterior maintains the basic architecture of a typical prewar apartment house, anchored by a four-story limestone base, warm wood-paneled lobby, and regularly spaced windows inserted into simple brick walls. The facade, however, is an odd mix of chamfered corners paired with aggressive offset tapering and vertical brick lines topped by sharp stone spikes between corner turrets, together bringing to mind a kind of Roaring Twenties ziggurat. Inside, the unique facade shapes the distinctive character of the 180 homes, with chamfered living rooms, high ceilings, and many spectacular terraces.

Its status as a hotel meant that 1 Fifth could be built taller than an apartment house, and the architects had a freer hand to blend architectural approaches without the classical constraints imposed upon the boxy prewars up the street. The building has earned its landmark status in New York, even featuring in the title of a novel by Candace Bushnell about the trappings of modern society, the Internet, and the art world.

39
FIFTH
AVENUE

GROSVENOR APARTMENTS

BEDROOM
10'-11" X 12'-9"

CL

W/D

BEDROOM
13'-11" X 10'-9"

CL

CL

CL

BEDROOM
17'-6" X 12'-9"

UPPER LEVEL

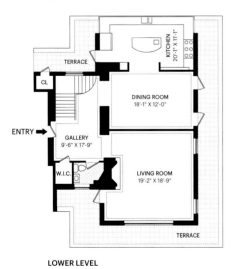

TERRACE

KITCHEN
20'-1" X 11'-1"

CL

DINING ROOM
18'-1" X 12'-0"

ENTRY ➡

GALLERY
9'-6" X 17'-9"

W.I.C.

LIVING ROOM
19'-2" X 18'-9"

TERRACE

LOWER LEVEL

40 FIFTH AVENUE

43
FIFTH
AVENUE

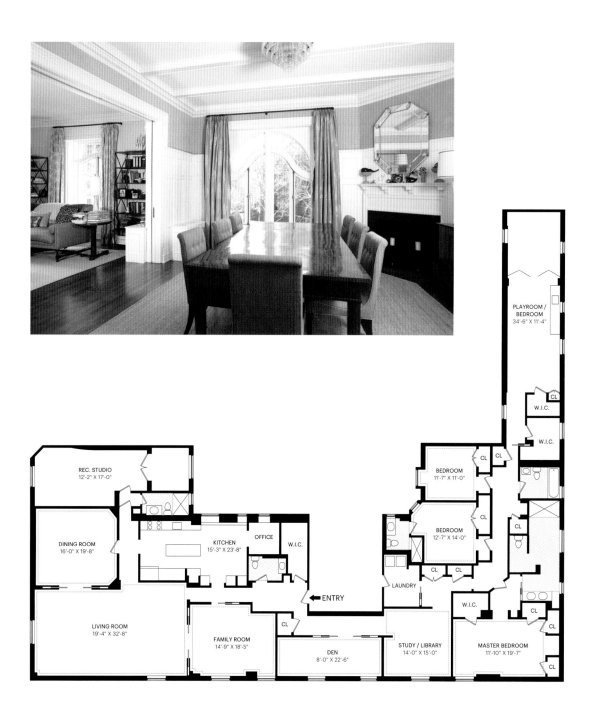

45 CHRISTOPHER STREET

BEDROOM
15'-4" X 12'-0"

LIVING ROOM
24'-9" X 13'-8"

W.I.C.

KITCHEN
12'-5" X 4'-10"

CL

CL   W.I.C.

ENTRY

2 HORATIO STREET

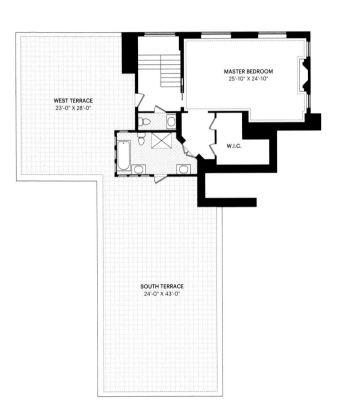

WEST TERRACE
23'-0" X 28'-0"

MASTER BEDROOM
25'-10" X 24'-10"

W.I.C.

SOUTH TERRACE
24'-0" X 43'-0"

UPPER LEVEL

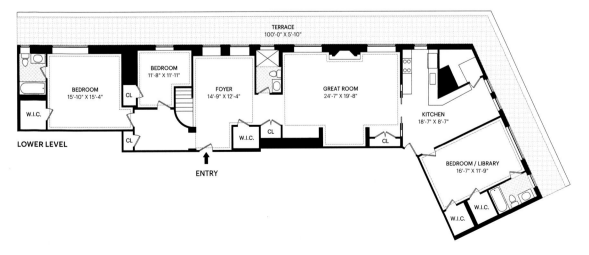

TERRACE
100'-0" X 5'-10"

BEDROOM
15'-10" X 15'-4"

W.I.C.

CL

BEDROOM
11'-8" X 11'-11"

CL

FOYER
14'-9" X 12'-4"

GREAT ROOM
24'-7" X 19'-8"

KITCHEN
18'-7" X 8'-7"

W.I.C.

CL

CL

LOWER LEVEL

ENTRY

BEDROOM / LIBRARY
16'-7" X 11'-9"

W.I.C.

W.I.C.

28
EAST 10TH
STREET

DEVONSHIRE HOUSE

BEDROOM
11'-4" X 14'-10"

LIBRARY / BEDROOM
21'-6" X 13'-0"

BEDROOM
11'-0" X 14'-4"

MASTER
BEDROOM
12'-4" X 19'-5"

CL

CL

CL

CL

CL

CL

W.I.C.

CL

CL

ENTRY   KITCHEN

DINING ROOM
12'-0" X 19'-6"

LIVING ROOM
20'-4" X 19'-6"

40–50 EAST 10TH STREET

BEDROOM
6'-6" X 17'-3"

BEDROOM
11'-6" X 18'-6"

FAMILY ROOM
14'-9" X 27'-3"

CL

CL

CL   CL

MASTER BEDROOM
16'-4" X 17'-6"

CL

CL

UPPER LEVEL

KITCHEN
11'-6" X 17'-6"

DINING ROOM
12'-9" X 17'-6"

LIVING ROOM
15'-9" X 27'-10"

LIBRARY
12'-0" X 17'-4"

FOYER

ENTRY ➡

CL

W.I.C.

LOWER LEVEL

59
WEST 12TH
STREET

ENTRY

CL

CL

BEDROOM
8'-10" X 7'-8"

LIVING ROOM
21'-9" X 11'-9"

KITCHEN
7'-5" X 9'-0"

242 EAST 19TH STREET

36 GRAMERCY PARK EAST

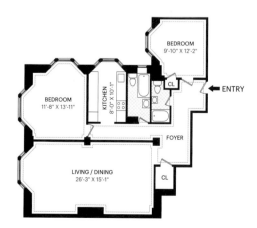

44 GRAMERCY PARK NORTH

LIVING ROOM
13'-9" X 25'-3"

BEDROOM
10'-8" X 12'-9"

W.I.C.

CL   CL

FOYER   STUDY

ENTRY →

KITCHEN
8'-7" X 6'-8"

60 GRAMERCY PARK NORTH

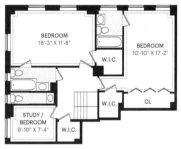

BEDROOM
18'-3" X 11'-8"

BEDROOM
10'-10" X 17'-2"

W.I.C.

W.I.C.

CL

STUDY /
BEDROOM
9'-10" X 7'-4"

W.I.C.

UPPER LEVEL

TERRACE
29'-5" X 24'-0"

DINING ROOM
15'-0" X 13'-5"

LIVING ROOM
20'-0" X 13'-5"

KITCHEN
9'-7" X 8'-8"

GALLERY
22'-0" X 6'-2"

W.I.C.

ENTRY

LOWER LEVEL

1 LEXINGTON AVENUE

MASTER BEDROOM
24'-0" X 12'-7"

BALCONY

BEDROOM
13'-7" X 10'-9"

CL

CL

CL

CL

CL

BEDROOM
12'-8" X 7'-6"

CL

UPPER LEVEL

LIVING ROOM
24'-0" X 14'-8"

DINING ROOM
20'-6" X 14'-7"

CL

KITCHEN
16'-7" X 10'-0"   FOYER

← ENTRY

BREAKFAST
ROOM
8'-0" X 6'-0"

LOWER LEVEL

In 1831 developer Samuel B. Ruggles proposed the idea of building a small, private neighborhood park just north of the growing city. He had bought from James Duane Gramercy Farm, which he would transform from part swamp, part field into what we know today as Gramercy Park. By 1833 a black cast-iron fence had been built and the park landscaped. It was bordered by sixty parcels of land that would each have a key to the park. Though the Panic of 1837 delayed construction of the first surrounding town houses, by the 1850s the area around the park began to look like a neighborhood.

The first apartment house to be built on Gramercy Park was the Indian-red brick 34 Gramercy Park, constructed on the southeast corner in 1881. It terrified neighbors, who thought it would topple over because it was so tall—nine stories was a skyscraper in those days. Next door, white terra-cotta-faced 36 Gramercy Park was built in 1909, with Gothic-inspired detailing, romantic cast-iron gas lamps lining the sidewalk, and a dramatic red carpet outside that leads to the front door.

Cyrus West Field had owned the house that 1 Lexington replaced. He was a financier who made his first fortune in paper manufacturing. By age thirty-four, when he moved into the neighborhood, he was one of the richest men in the city. In the 1850s he became a patron of Hudson River School painter Frederic Edwin Church, financing the expeditions into the Andes that would inspire some of Church's greatest works, including the 5-foot-long *The Heart of the Andes*, in the collection of the Metropolitan Museum of Art. An impatient entrepreneur looking for further business adventures, Field financed the first transatlantic telegraph cable in 1858, along with Peter Cooper, his friend and neighbor. Though Field died in bankruptcy, he revolutionized the speed of international communication between Europe and the United States. What once took three to four weeks to send by mail on a ship took seconds by telegraph.

With twenty-eight homes spread over twelve floors, 1 Lexington Avenue was architect Herbert Lucas's second building on the square. The dark-brown brick 24 Gramercy Park, topped by a bright-green copper cornice and curved wrought iron balconies, was completed in 1909, the same year as Lucas's 535 Park Avenue. All three buildings have in common sizable apartments, and each has a number of very houselike duplexes. Apartments in 1 Lexington feature a front hall with a stair, a living room facing the park, a dining room farther back, and typically three bedrooms upstairs. This configuration was easy to sell, as almost all well-off families lived in town houses at the time, so the change in lifestyle was minimal. It was known as a "club" building that offered families the amenities of a home without the headaches of maintaining their own building.

Its narrow balconies, particularly the one that wraps the eleventh floor, were not intended as real outdoor space, but instead to allow tall windows to extend almost to the floor inside, making rooms brighter and ceilings seem higher. Views from south-facing homes are outstanding, looking over the wavy green blanket of treetops in the square below and all the way down Irving Place to Fourteenth Street. These apartments have attracted notable residents such as actors Uma Thurman and Winona Ryder and restaurateur Danny Meyer.[17]

LONDON TERRACE

If the *Titanic* had been parked on Twenty-Third Street between Ninth and Tenth Avenues, it would have been just a little bigger than London Terrace. Finished in 1931, with 1,670 units, it was by far the world's largest apartment building to date. What is truly remarkable for a building of such colossal scale is how the blend of Spanish and Italian Romanesque Revival architecture, dotted with small shops, manicured gardens, and separate entrances, makes it such a pleasure to walk past. London Terrace yields a completely unexpected intimacy, particularly on its quieter Twenty-Fourth Street side. Sharp-eared gargoyles occupy the building's street corners, and spiraling columns frame entrances, while the three-story base switches between stone with arched windows at its ends to bands of colored brick in the center.

London Terrace is actually twelve separate side-by-side buildings, together forming a traditional courtyard building. Two twenty-story tapered towers are the bookends, facing Ninth and Tenth Avenues with impressive views over Chelsea and to the Hudson River. In between are ten twelve-story buildings, each topped with a Tuscan-style water-tank enclosure. To attract residents and take advantage of the project's immense size and far-west location, all the basic services residents needed were included in the original buildings—a barber, a grocery store, a pharmacy, a few restaurants, and the largest enclosed swimming pool in the city. Doormen were dressed as London bobbies. A "Marine Deck" on the twentieth floor, mimicking the design of a luxury ocean liner, had a gym, club, and rooftop children's play area. Over the years the courtyard

has grown in, sporting a thick green fur of vines that climb the once-bare brick walls, surrounding rows of trees and a garden path.

Developer Henry Mandel was the Donald Trump of the late 1920s. Bold and flashy, he became bored with the tenements he built with his father early in his career. He opened the massive Parc Vendome apartment house on West Fifty-Seventh Street in 1931, and 895 and 898 Park Avenue were also his. He had dreams of building apartment houses on every corner of Seventh Avenue between Sixteenth and Twenty-Second Streets, but ended up constructing only a few, including 201 West Sixteenth Street. London Terrace was his prized project—a building bigger than anything else in town.

Just weeks before the 1929 stock market crash, Mandel's construction crews finished clearing the block-long site for London Terrace. New York real estate development demands nerves of steel and an exceedingly thick skin; undeterred by the financial uncertainty, Mandel pushed forward, and by the following year the ten central buildings had risen. Another year later, the almost unimaginably big building was complete. But by 1932 the Great Depression had caught up with Mandel's overconfidence, forcing him into bankruptcy. Unable to pay his ex-wife's alimony, he ended up in jail the following year.

Farrar & Watmaugh, also Mandel's architects for the taller Parc Vendome, stocked the London Terrace buildings with hundreds of well-proportioned studios and one-bedrooms, knowing that families preferred instead to live uptown near Central Park. Though small, each has a foyer and walk-in closets, and even the studios have a separate dressing room. B-line one-bedrooms have huge 20-by-14-foot living rooms with a fireplace. A-lines have four closets. There are some two-bedrooms, along with three-bedroom penthouses. Light, views, and access to the Hudson River Park now make the building highly desirable. It is also hard-to-miss proof that very large apartment buildings don't have to look like lifeless housing projects, disconnected from the surrounding street life.

ACKNOWLEDGMENTS

You have absolutely no idea how much work goes into publishing a book, nor understand the need for a highly skilled team, until you've gone through the process. To bring this historical building type back to life in color took a very dedicated group of people who recognized the beauty and architectural importance of prewar apartment homes.

Without such generosity, prompt replies, and remarkable kindness, this book never would have happened. The team at Princeton Architectural Press has been absolutely superb. Kevin Lippert gave the book a chance when Hugh Hardy graciously brought a previous version by his office. Jennifer Lippert gently steered it in the right direction, while Sara Stemen's dedication, patience, and drive managing the project brought the idea to life. Elana Schlenker's book design perfectly captures the essence of the prewar apartment, and Meredith Baber's diligence in seeking out the rich color photography has been invaluable.

Center-hall floor plans are the very source of prewar beauty. David Haakenson meticulously crafted one for each building, and I hope in doing so began to understand my passion for these old buildings, even though we work on striking modern ones at the office.

The real estate brokers and photographers who gave their time to hunt down or provide photographs are due my sincere gratitude. The color photography is what readers yearn for, to bring these one-hundred-year-old buildings to life.

My parents encouraged me not to buy a TV when I moved into my own apartment. I'm grateful for many things, but because I had no choice but to explore New York during the day and had evenings free to type, the roots of the book took shape. And finally, my lovely wife Carmela's endless patience and support meant she joined me even on the coldest days of the winter to help take photographs. I watched her fall in love with a street-level prewar on 100th Street by Riverside Park: I cannot thank her enough here.

PREWAR ARCHITECTS

GEORGE & EDWARD BLUM

GEORGE BLUM (1870–1928)

EDWARD BLUM (1876–1944)

Red brick and limestone are the staples of apartment house construction in New York, so anyone passing 780 West End Avenue, covered head to toe in bright white terra-cotta, might wonder if its architects designed any other such buildings. Fortunately, the answer is yes; a journey around Manhattan uncovers a fascinating body of work by a firm that steered clear of the conventional classical mold to explore colorful terra-cotta, deliberately avoiding what everyone else was doing.

Brothers George and Edward Blum were prolific, but have largely been forgotten by history. After both studied at the École des Beaux-Arts, they opened their own firm in 1909 with a commission for 539 West 112th Street, the Phaeton. By 1917—five years before Rosario Candela completed his first building—they had completed an astonishing forty-five. The Blum brothers designed nine buildings on West End Avenue and eight on Park Avenue, although most of their work is found on side streets. A more subdued street presence is exhibited by 610 West End Avenue, but the building contains unexpectedly vast homes. More like 780 West End Avenue is 840 Park Avenue, which appears rebellious as an almost-white building in a sea of muted earth tones.

The gigantic Gramercy House, at 235 East Twenty-Second Street (a few blocks from Gramercy Park), was where the Blums let loose a little. Designed for Albert and Charles Mayer and William Korn, the building displays the Blum brothers' mix of aqua-green and mustard-yellow terra-cotta tiles, combined with polished chrome front doors. The blast of color continues around the second floor in a zigzag that weaves in between burnt-orange window frames. Few buildings were this daring (with the exception of Ely Jacques Kahn's 2 Park Avenue, about ten blocks away).

The Blums' very decorative terra-cotta facades are delicate, in need of a watchful eye and steady maintenance. However, even if a general conformity among prewar architects produced thousands of apartment homes that the public adores, it was significant that some went against the mold. Perhaps it was due to the Blum brothers' influence that Rosario Candela, Charles Platt, and Schwartz & Gross each began to veer away from classical traditions to explore new architectural ideas, leading to modern masterpieces such as 19 East Seventy-Second Street, 740 Park Avenue, and 120 East End Avenue.

ROSARIO CANDELA
(1890–1953)

Rosario Candela's buildings have, since the 1930s, steadily become the standard-bearers for the New York luxury apartment house. Candela's mastery of the center-hall floor plan, particularly the duplex, transformed the apartment house into an equal of the finest mansions, and his work advanced to the forefront of urban glamour. Because of his ability to craft highly individual and beautiful homes within the cramped confines of each property, his process led to architecturally distinctive and at times very dramatic buildings.

Born in Montelepre, Sicily, Candela immigrated with his family to the United States in 1906. By the time he was forty, Candela had designed some of the most sought-after apartment houses in Manhattan, in numerous locations overlooking Central Park and on Park Avenue. Spectacular duplex and triplex penthouses welcome visitors arriving from a private elevator into a grand entry foyer perhaps 40 feet long and 10 feet wide, which frames a curved stair leading to an upper floor. From there, tall doorways lead to palatial entertaining spaces where guests can flow from one room to the next throughout an evening. The foyer is the heart of the center-hall plan, just like in a private house, announcing a family's social status and marking its arrival home every day. Among Candela's finest works are 720, 740, and 778 Park Avenue, as well as 834, 960, and 1040 Fifth Avenue.

During his brief burst of genius through the 1920s, when he designed most of his buildings, Candela created a rich legacy of apartment houses even beyond the most prestigious addresses. West End Avenue has nine of his buildings, and much of Sutton Place is his work, with the side streets of the Upper West Side boasting even more examples. Candela's touch for the center-hall plan is apparent even in his more modest buildings, evident the moment you enter the apartments: 800 West End Avenue, 325 and 334 West Eighty-Sixth Street, and 40 West Sixty-Seventh Street are each delightful. Candela also designed a few buildings outside Manhattan; there are two overlooking Grand Army Plaza in Brooklyn and one in Chicago.

J. E. R. CARPENTER
(1867–1932)

J. E. R. Carpenter's rich portfolio of work is lesser known than either Emery Roth's or Rosario Candela's because it rarely strayed outside the borders of the Upper East Side. Eighteen of his apartment houses are on Fifth Avenue facing Central Park, and another thirteen are on Park Avenue. His architecture very deliberately does not draw much attention to itself or its residents; instead, Carpenter created homes that in many ways defined understated elegance. Visually lighter than some of his contemporaries' work and avoiding strong architectural features such as spires and aggressive ornament surrounding the front door, his work established the quiet and elegant, though highly refined, tone of both avenues.

After studying at the University of Tennessee, MIT, and the École des Beaux-Arts, Carpenter received his first commission in 1909, for a nine-story apartment house at 116 East Fifty-Eighth Street. He exhibited a remarkable level of resolution for a young architect, and his work quickly grew in size and prominence. In 1912 950 Park Avenue was completed, and 246 West End Avenue in 1913. Four more on Park Avenue would soon follow—numbers 635, 640, 630, and 550— as well as 907 Fifth Avenue, before World War I slowed the apartment house market.

During the construction boom of the Roaring Twenties, Carpenter would complete an extraordinary thirty-three new apartment houses, including all but one of his Fifth Avenue commissions. Full-floor homes such as those in 810, 950, 988, and 1030 Fifth (the last especially enormous) were a specialty. A lovely departure from his typical use of spare limestone walls is 655 Park Avenue, a low-rise Georgian courtyard building. But the jewel of Riverside Drive, number 173–175 (completed in 1927), is perhaps his finest piece of architecture. Carpenter quietly added extra charm, emphasizing the design's gentle curve, freed from the typical box, with strong horizontal bands. Narrow stone spirals soften the corners, paired with shallow balconies that add depth. Sheathed in limestone and buff brick, like 1165 and 1170 Fifth Avenue, it is a pleasure to pass at street level, yet maintains a commanding presence on the drive. Inside, the homes are his most interesting mix of sizes, arranged in a complex and brilliant three-dimensional puzzle.

CHARLES PLATT
(1861–1933)

Charles Platt's apartment house architecture can be austere, merging an understated elegance with rigid adherence to grids and order. Yet it reveals an exceedingly fine touch, pairing skillfully balanced proportions with concentrated doses of ornament, as exemplified in his design for the entranceways at 131–135 East Sixty-Sixth Street. Minimal but muscular, his design approach transformed the apartment house box into an object of high luxury. He also had a passion for landscape architecture, which he incorporated into the magnificent estates he designed for the Pratt family residence in Glen Cove, Long Island, and the Francis T. Maxwell House, perched on a hillside in Vernon, Connecticut.

The Astor family was Platt's primary apartment house patron, hiring him for three of his four buildings (the exception being 131–135 East Sixty-Sixth Street). Overlooking Carl Schurz Park at the river's edge of East Eighty-Sixth Street, 120 East End Avenue is a seventeen-story sheer cliff of pale limestone. Templelike with its flat facade, the building contains sprawling homes with large floor-to-ceiling windows; it was remarkably modern without embracing the art deco trend. It was completed in 1931 at the sunset of the great apartment house era, a time when the architectural community was finally working itself free of the confines of classical ornament.

Around the corner are twins 520 and 530 East Eighty-Sixth Street, two modest, reddish-brown brick buildings with unexpectedly large homes inside. Some apartments have the beautiful bay windows you'd expect in a town house. Massive 131–135 East Sixty-Sixth Street is coveted for its 20-foot-tall living rooms and Juliet balconies. Across town at Astor Court (205 West Eighty-Ninth Street), beautiful and sizable B-line and H-line homes have six or seven rooms each. Its garden has recently been restored, and the lobby overlooking it, with its sea of white marble and brass detailing, immediately brings to mind why prewars are so desirable.

EMERY ROTH
(1871–1948)

Emery Roth's three iconic apartment houses on Central Park West—the San Remo, the Beresford, and the Eldorado—are among the most photographed spires of the New York skyline. Their soaring towers stand as trophies to the grand aspirations, drive, and growth of 1920s New York.

By necessity, apartment houses are usually boxes, no matter who designs them. Plans are designed to maximize the number of apartments and floor area for a given piece of property. Roth was well known by real estate developers for providing accurate floor areas and material quantities throughout the design process, so that they could manage costs and choose where to invest in design. His signature design approach was to locate the building-code-required water tank on the roof and then design a grand enclosure for it, transforming it into a spire. Roth understood the role the roofline plays on the skyline, and used height to underscore his buildings' civic prominence.

Roth was born in Sečovce, now in Slovakia. He was sent to the United States alone when he was thirteen because his mother could not afford to keep him after his father died. Roth began his architectural apprenticeship in the Chicago office of Burnham & Root. Impressed by the young architect, Richard Morris

Hunt hired him away to work in New York, and Roth subsequently started his own practice.

Although Roth was one of the era's most prolific architects, his work has remained somewhat in the shadows of Rosario Candela's, perhaps because of the concentration of prominent residents in Candela's 740 and 778 Park Avenue and now 834 Fifth Avenue. It was Roth who first conceived of the skyscraper apartment house, with the completion of the 1925 Ritz Tower at the prominent corner of East Fifty-Seventh Street and Park Avenue. He went on to champion the tower as the future of residential design, and his center-hall floor plans are consistently stellar. His designs for 15 West Eighty-First Street and 993 Fifth Avenue are exquisite, and some of his lesser-known works, such as 242 East Nineteenth Street, 221 West Eighty-Second Street, 333 and 580 West End Avenue, and 59 West Twelfth Street (Jimi Hendrix's former home), are equally remarkable.

SCHWARTZ & GROSS
SIMON I. SCHWARTZ (1877–1956)
ARTHUR GROSS (1877–1950)

Schwartz & Gross was so prolific and its work so diverse, it's hard to identify its apartment houses by a particular style or recognizable feature. The firm designed hundreds of apartment houses throughout Manhattan, yet without any major landmarks such as museums on its résumé, its enormous contribution to the city has been largely unappreciated. By designing so many buildings (often before Roth or Candela did on major streets and avenues), Schwartz & Gross established the design fundamentals for the proud, pleasant, and warm architectural tone of stone and brick that characterizes the Upper West and Upper East Sides.

Eight of its buildings are on Central Park West, at least twelve on Riverside Drive, twenty-two on West End Avenue, and eighteen on Park Avenue. Its prized works include the Gothic-inspired courtyard apartment house 1185 Park Avenue and the art deco 55 Central Park West. The twin curved facades of 435 and 440 Riverside Drive mark the beginning of West 116th Street, which leads to the gates of Columbia University, and 845 West End Avenue has recently been restored to its original splendor.

In Washington Heights, Schwartz & Gross designed the Grinnell (800 Riverside Drive), completed in 1911. Nicknamed the "Dakota of the north," it sits on a rare triangular footprint; few know of this building, with its enormous and bright homes, situated in the Audubon Park Historic District.

SUGARMAN & BERGER
HENRY M. SUGARMAN (1888–1946)
A. G. BERGER (DATES UNKNOWN)

Sugarman & Berger is best known for the massive art deco New Yorker Hotel at Eighth Avenue and Thirty-Fourth Street, notable on the skyline for its three-story-tall sign. The firm was founded in 1926, at the height of the Roaring Twenties building frenzy.

Wedding cake–shaped skyscrapers were its strength, exemplified by two apartment houses, One Fifth Avenue and 310 Riverside Drive. Both were designed with Helmle, Corbett & Harrison. One Fifth Avenue is a soaring twenty-seven-story landmark towering over the tidy rows of town houses around Washington Square Park in Greenwich Village. Chamfered corners paired with innumerable setbacks are topped by a needle-point spire, evoking a giant aerodynamic machine with its own radio transmitter. The Master Apartments at 310 Riverside Drive gathered the same architectural collaborators to design a residential hotel with a street-level museum for the Russian-born artist Nicholas Roerich. The building stands out from the flat-topped, curving apartment houses on either side, ensuring spectacular views from its upper floors and duplex penthouse. A few blocks farther north is 340 Riverside Drive, perched on a bluff at the end of 106th Street. Its B-line homes also have magnificent views of the Hudson River and Riverside Park.

SELECTED BUILDINGS
BY ARCHITECT

Gaetano Ajello

West End Avenue

473 West End Avenue

505 West End Avenue

512 West End Avenue

575 West End Avenue

645 West End Avenue

884 West End Avenue

885 West End Avenue

895 West End Avenue

905 West End Avenue

Riverside Drive

160 Riverside Drive

360 Riverside Drive

375 Riverside Drive

390 Riverside Drive

395 Riverside Drive

420 Riverside Drive

West Side

235 West 71st Street

305 West 72nd Street

Henry Anderson

Fifth Avenue

43 Fifth Avenue

West Side

137 Central Park North

Grosvenor Atterbury

Downtown

4 Lexington Avenue

George A. Bagge & Sons

West Side

173 West 78th Street

G. B. Beaumont

East Side

31 East 79th Street

Bien & Prince

East Side

35 East 76th Street

Bing & Bing (developers)

Park Avenue

417 Park Avenue

565 Park Avenue

570 Park Avenue

784 Park Avenue

903 Park Avenue

960 Park Avenue

970 Park Avenue

993 Park Avenue

1000 Park Avenue

1009 Park Avenue

1155 Park Avenue

East Side

140 East 28th Street

433 East 51st Street

400 East 52nd Street

414 East 52nd Street

424 East 52nd Street

444 East 52nd Street

45 East 66th Street

233 East 72nd Street

245 East 72nd Street

204–206 East 73rd Street

210 East 73rd Street

215 East 73rd Street

220 East 73rd Street

225 East 73rd Street

230 East 73rd Street

235 East 73rd Street

224 East 74th Street

232 East 74th Street

240 East 74th Street

252–254 East 74th Street

129 East 82nd Street

64–66 East 83rd Street

West Side

162 West 56th Street

312 West 71st Street

225 Central Park West

235 West End Avenue

601 West End Avenue

Downtown

2 Horatio Street

45 Christopher Street

59 West 12th Street

299 West 12th Street

302 West 12th Street

Charles E. Birge

West End Avenue

945 West End Avenue

Riverside Drive

137 Riverside Drive

George & Edward Blum

Park Avenue

555 Park Avenue

791 Park Avenue

830 Park Avenue

840 Park Avenue

875 Park Avenue

929 Park Avenue

940 Park Avenue

1075 Park Avenue

East Side

138/144 East 36th Street

145 East 49th Street

405 East 54th Street

360 East 55th Street

320 East 57th Street

419 East 57th Street

210 East 68th Street

315 East 68th Street

101 East 74th Street

156 East 79th Street

12 East 87th Street

150 East 93rd Street

865 First Avenue

1435 Lexington Ave

Central Park West

322 Central Park West

West End Avenue

277 West End Avenue

599 West End Avenue

610 West End Avenue

617 West End Avenue

670 West End Avenue

760 West End Avenue

780 West End Avenue

828 West End Avenue

838 West End Avenue

Riverside Drive

454 Riverside Drive

West Side

200 West 54th Street

105 West 72nd Street

166 West 72nd Street

244 West 72nd Street

330 West 72nd Street

120 West 86th Street

326 West 86th Street

251 West 89th Street

207 West 98th Street

215 West 98th Street

241 West 108th Street

545 West 111th Street

539 West 112th Street

535 West 113th Street

601 West 113th Street

Downtown

235 East 22nd Street

Boak & Paris

East Side

227 East 57th Street

177 East 77th Street

50 East 78th Street

5 West 86th Street

110 East 87th Street

152 East 94th Street

Riverside Drive

5 Riverside Drive

100 Riverside Drive

315 Riverside Drive

West End Avenue

336 West End Avenue

450 West End Avenue

West Side

127 West 96th Street

225 West 106th Street

444 Central Park West

Downtown

302 West 12th Street

Albert Joseph Bodker

Central Park West

333 Central Park West

George A. & Henry Boehm

Downtown

45 Gramercy Park North

Alfred C. Bossom

Riverside Drive

355 Riverside Drive

William Lawrence Bottomley

Downtown

1 Gracie Square (with Rosario Candela)

Bottomley, Wagner & White

East Side

435 East 52nd Street

William Boring

Park Avenue

520 Park Avenue

521 Park Avenue

540 Park Avenue

Rosario Candela

Fifth Avenue

2 East 64th Street

834 Fifth Avenue

2 East 67th Street

2 East 70th Street

955 Fifth Avenue

960 Fifth Avenue (with Warren & Wetmore)

990 Fifth Avenue (with Warren & Wetmore)

1040 Fifth Avenue

Park Avenue

720 Park Avenue (with Cross & Cross)

740 Park Avenue (with Arthur Loomis Harmon)

765/775 Park Avenue

770 Park Avenue

778 Park Avenue

1021 Park Avenue

1105 Park Avenue

1172 Park Avenue

1192 Park Avenue

1220 Park Avenue

East Side

130 East 39th Street

248 East 46th Street

2 Beekman Place

135 East 54th Street

120 East 56th Street

340 East 57th Street

447 East 57th Street

40 East 66th Street

44 East 67th Street

19 East 72nd Street (with Mott B. Schmidt)

133 East 80th Street

1 Gracie Square (with William Law Bottomley)

12 East 88th Street

70 East 96th Street

8 East 96th Street

19 East 98th Street

Sutton Place

4 Sutton Place

25 Sutton Place

30 Sutton Place

1 Sutton Place South

14 Sutton Place South

Central Park West

75 Central Park West

360 Central Park West

280 Riverside Drive

285 Riverside Drive

425 Riverside Drive

West End Avenue

230 West End Avenue

240 West End Avenue

320 West End Avenue

522 West End Avenue

607 West End Avenue

755 West End Avenue

800 West End Avenue

820 West End Avenue

875 West End Avenue

878 West End Avenue

915 West End Avenue

West Side

40 West 55th Street

127 West 57th Street

307 West 57th Street

100 West 58th Street

150 West 58th Street

40 West 67th Street

161 West 75th Street

325 West 86th Street

334 West 86th Street

175 West 89th Street

304 West 89th Street

215 West 92nd Street

315 West 106th Street

300 West 108th Street

Downtown

56 Seventh Avenue

41 Fifth Avenue

Brooklyn

39 Plaza Street West

47 Plaza Street West

Carrère & Hastings

East Side

109 East 57th Street

J. E. R. Carpenter

Fifth Avenue

810 Fifth Avenue

825 Fifth Avenue

845 Fifth Avenue

907 Fifth Avenue

920 Fifth Avenue

950 Fifth Avenue

988 Fifth Avenue

1030 Fifth Avenue

1035 Fifth Avenue

1060 Fifth Avenue

1070 Fifth Avenue

1115 Fifth Avenue

1120 Fifth Avenue

1143 Fifth Avenue

1148 Fifth Avenue

1150 Fifth Avenue

1165 Fifth Avenue

1170 Fifth Avenue

Park Avenue

550 Park Avenue

580 Park Avenue

610 Park Avenue

620 Park Avenue

625 Park Avenue

630 Park Avenue

635 Park Avenue

640 Park Avenue

655 Park Avenue (with Mott B. Schmidt)

812 Park Avenue

950 Park Avenue

960 Park Avenue

1050 Park Avenue

1060 Park Avenue

East Side

145 East 52nd Street

116 East 58th Street

5 East 73rd Street

145 East 73rd Street

170 East 79th Street

115 East 82nd Street

3 East 85th Street

14 East 90th Street

4 East 95th Street

Riverside Drive

173–175 Riverside Drive

West End Avenue

246 West End Avenue

West Side

30 Central Park South

112 Central Park South

Walter B. Chambers

Fifth Avenue

1148 Fifth Avenue

Park Avenue

563 Park Avenue

Irwin S. Chanin

Central Park West

25 Central Park West

115 Central Park West (with Jacques Delamarre)

H. O. Chapman

Fifth Avenue

952 Fifth Avenue

Clinton & Russell

Central Park West

135 Central Park West

West Side

235 West 75th Street

2211 Broadway

1923 Seventh Avenue

Crane & Franzheim

Fifth Avenue

1158 Fifth Avenue

Cross & Cross

Park Avenue

720 Park Avenue (with Rosario Candela)

East Side

25 East End Avenue

George W. DaCunha

Downtown

34 Gramercy Park East

Jacques Delamarre

Central Park West

115 Central Park West (with Irwin S. Chanin)

Delano & Aldrich

Park Avenue

925 Park Avenue

1040 Park Avenue

Denby & Nute

Riverside Drive

417 Riverside Drive

De Pace & Juster

Park Avenue

1100 Park Avenue

Maurice Deutsch

Riverside Drive

150 Riverside Drive

Deutsch & Schneider

Riverside Drive

52 Riverside Drive

F. H. Dewey & Co.

Park Avenue

510 Park Avenue

Ditmars & Brite

West Side

11 West 81st Street

Paul E. M. Duboy

West Side

2109 Broadway (with W. E. D. Stokes)

Ellis, Aaronson & Heidrich

East Side

301 East 38th Street

229 East 79th Street

West Side

27 West 96th Street

Farrar & Watmaugh

Downtown

200 West 16th Street

201 West 16th Street

405–465 West 23rd Street

470 West 24th Street

Jacob M. Felson

Park Avenue

975 Park Avenue

East Side

308 East 79th Street

19 East 80th Street

140 East 81st Street

40 East 86th Street

430 East 86th Street

Central Park West

350 Central Park West

West End Avenue

515 West End Avenue

697 West End Avenue

900 West End Avenue

West Side

230 Central Park South

40 West 77th Street

201 West 85th Street

107 West 86th Street

114 West 86th Street

115 West 86th Street

144 West 86th Street

145 West 86th Street

220 West 93rd Street

Downtown

301 East 21st Street

William B. Franke

West End Avenue

401 West End Avenue

Frederick F. French

Fifth Avenue

1010 Fifth Avenue

1140 Fifth Avenue

East Side

Tudor City

Cass P. H. Gilbert

Fifth Avenue

1067 Fifth Avenue

Goldner & Goldner

West End Avenue

393 West End Avenue

West Side

211 West 106th Street

Lafayette A. Goldstone

East Side

442 East 57th Street

4 East 72nd Street

50 East 72nd Street

James Riely Gordon

Downtown

36 Gramercy Park East

Graves & Duboy

West Side

2109 Broadway

Gronenberg & Leuchtag

Park Avenue

1230 Park Avenue

1235 Park Avenue

East Side

45 East 30th Street

145 East 74th Street

179 East 79th Street

325 East 79th Street

Central Park West

467 Central Park West

West End Avenue

235 West End Avenue

639 West End Avenue

Riverside Drive

50 Riverside Drive

110 Riverside Drive

118 Riverside Drive

West Side

17 West 67th Street

124 West 79th Street

25 West 81st Street

130 West 86th Street

315 West 86th Street

201 West 92nd Street

145 West 96th Street

245 West 104th Street

Downtown

100 Waverly Place

Walter Haefeli

West End Avenue

562 West End Avenue

Harde & Short

West Side

180 West 58th Street

44 West 77th Street

Julius Harder

Park Avenue

410 Park Avenue

Arthur Loomis Harmon

Park Avenue

740 Park Avenue (with Rosario Candela)

Helmle & Corbett

Downtown

29–45 East 9th Street

Helmle, Corbett & Harrison

Riverside Drive

310 Riverside Drive (with Sugarman & Berger)

Downtown

1 Fifth Avenue (with Sugarman & Berger)

40–50 East 10th Street

Henry J. Hardenbergh

West Side

1 West 72nd Street

Arthur Paul Hess

Park Avenue

891 Park Avenue

1049 Park Avenue

Downtown

200 East 16th Street

Hiss & Weekes

West Side

225 West 86th Street

Hoffman & Goldstone

Park Avenue

730 Park Avenue

Horgan & Slattery

East Side

667 Madison Avenue

Hubert, Pirsson & Company

East Side

80 Madison Avenue

121 Madison Avenue

The Hawthorne (Address Unknown)

The Hubert (Address Unknown)

The Navarro (Central Park South between Sixth & Seventh Avenues)

Richard Morris Hunt

Downtown

142 East 18th Street

H. Douglas Ives

East Side

Tudor City

Harry Allan Jacobs

Park Avenue

820 Park Avenue

Ely Jacques Kahn

Park Avenue

2 Park Avenue

Leo F. Knust

West End Avenue

677 West End Avenue

West Side

12 West 96th Street

Nathan Korn

Fifth Avenue

944 Fifth Avenue

956 Fifth Avenue

Park Avenue

1133 Park Avenue

Central Park West

230 Central Park West

327 Central Park West

West Side

6–16 West 77th Street

850 Amsterdam Avenue

Thomas W. Lamb

Fifth Avenue

51 Fifth Avenue

East Side

49 East 96th Street

Lawlor & Haase

Riverside Drive

305 Riverside Drive

Electus D. Litchfield

East Side

79 East 79th Street

Electus D. Litchfield & Pliny Rogers

Park Avenue

800 Park Avenue

Arthur Lobo

West End Avenue

736 West End Avenue

Herbert Lucas

Park Avenue

535 Park Avenue

Downtown

1 Lexington Avenue

Robert T. Lyons

Park Avenue

565 Park Avenue

903 Park Avenue

955 Park Avenue

993 Park Avenue

1155 Park Avenue

Central Park West

285 Central Park West

535 West 110th Street

Downtown

245 East 21st Street

2 Horatio Street

Evan T. MacDonald

Riverside Drive

299 Riverside Drive

Margon & Holder

Fifth Avenue

965 Fifth Avenue

Central Park West

300 Central Park West (with Emery Roth)

410 Central Park West

West Side

49 West 72nd Street

200 West 86th Street

400 West End Avenue

Margon & Glaser

Park Avenue

77 Park Avenue

McKim, Mead & White

Fifth Avenue

998 Fifth Avenue

Park Avenue

277 Park Avenue

East Side

1 East End Avenue

Downtown

40 Fifth Avenue (with Van Wart & Wein)

Herman Lee Meader

Riverside Drive

243 Riverside Drive

George G. Miller

West Side

35 West 92nd Street

Mulliken & Moeller

Central Park West

251 Central Park West

257 Central Park West

West End Avenue

530 West End Avenue

West Side

175 West 72nd Street

170 West 73rd Street

201 West 79th Street

302 West 86th Street

320 West 86th Street

267 West 89th Street

Kenneth Murchison

East Side

133 East 64th Street

844 Lexington Avenue

160 East 72nd Street

Nast & Springsteen

West End Avenue

782 West End Avenue

Neville & Bagge

Central Park West

293 Central Park West

West End Avenue

325 West End Avenue

490 West End Avenue

498 West End Avenue

590 West End Avenue

789 West End Avenue

801 West End Avenue

817 West End Avenue

Riverside Drive

131 Riverside Drive

410 Riverside Drive

West Side

35 West 81st Street

H. Thomas O'Hara

Riverside Drive

230 Riverside Drive

George F. Pelham

Fifth Avenue

575 Fifth Avenue

944 Fifth Avenue

1136 Fifth Avenue

1240 Fifth Avenue

Park Avenue

575 Park Avenue

944 Park Avenue

1120 Park Avenue

1160 Park Avenue

1225 Park Avenue

1240 Park Avenue

East Side

136 East 64th Street

135 East 74th Street

115 East 86th Street

Central Park West

325 Central Park West

West End Avenue

270 West End Avenue

441 West End Avenue

470 West End Avenue

545 West End Avenue

585 West End Avenue

675 West End Avenue

710 West End Avenue

910 West End Avenue

Riverside Drive

33 Riverside Drive

98 Riverside Drive

290 Riverside Drive

West Side

20 West 77th Street

164 West 79th Street

175 West 79th Street

10 West 86th Street

140 West 86th Street

50 West 96th Street

Downtown

81 Irving Place

George F. Pelham Jr.

Park Avenue

1130 Park Avenue

Henry C. Pelton

Park Avenue

1035 Park Avenue

Pennington, Lewis & Mills

Fifth Avenue

1068 Fifth Avenue

Park Avenue

1001 Park Avenue

East Side

1 East End Avenue

10 Gracie Square

John B. Peterkin

Fifth Avenue

1016 Fifth Avenue

Pickering & Walker

Park Avenue

823/829 Park Avenue

969 Park Avenue

Charles Platt

East Side

131–135 East 66th Street

520/530 East 86th Street

120 East End Avenue

West Side

205 West 89th Street

George Mort Pollard

West Side

1 West 67th Street

Pollard & Steinem

Park Avenue

863 Park Avenue

West Side

257 West 86th Street

Joseph L. Raimist

Fifth Avenue

969 Fifth Avenue

Rich & Mathesius

Central Park West

70 Central Park West

Charles W. Romeyn

Central Park West

50 Central Park West

Emery Roth

Fifth Avenue

875 Fifth Avenue

880 Fifth Avenue

930 Fifth Avenue

993 Fifth Avenue

1125 Fifth Avenue

1133 Fifth Avenue

1200 Fifth Avenue

Park Avenue

7 Park Avenue

20 Park Avenue

417 Park Avenue

455 Park Avenue

480 Park Avenue

570 Park Avenue

784 Park Avenue

1000 Park Avenue

1009 Park Avenue

1112 Park Avenue

1175 Park Avenue

East Side

140 East 28th Street

109 East 57th Street

435 East 57th Street

30 East 60th Street

210 East 73rd Street

215 East 73rd Street

220 East 73rd Street

225 East 73rd Street

230 East 73rd Street

235 East 73rd Street

151 East 80th Street

129 East 82nd Street

114 East 90th Street

60 East 96th Street

130 East End Avenue

Central Park West

65 Central Park West

145–146 Central Park West

211 Central Park West

225 Central Park West

275 Central Park West

295 Central Park West

300 Central Park West

320 Central Park West

West End Avenue

243 West End Avenue

310 West End Avenue

333 West End Avenue

580 West End Avenue

601 West End Avenue

720 West End Avenue

825 West End Avenue

Riverside Drive

140 Riverside Drive

186 Riverside Drive

West Side

228 West 71st Street

12 West 72nd Street

175 West 76th Street

118 West 79th Street

145 West 79th Street

15 West 81st Street

221 West 82nd Street

222 West 83rd Street

110 West 86th Street

201 West 89th Street

200 West 90th Street

41 West 96th Street

210 West 101st Street

Downtown

10 Sheridan Square

45 Christopher Street

1 University Place

24 Fifth Avenue

39 Fifth Avenue

28 East 10th Street

164 2nd Avenue

59 West 12th Street

299 West 12th Street

242 East 19th Street

200 West 20th Street

60 Gramercy Park North

300 West 23rd Street

Brooklyn

35 Prospect Park West

William L. Rouse

Riverside Drive

258 Riverside Drive

380 Riverside Drive

Rouse & Goldstone

Fifth Avenue

1107 Fifth Avenue

Park Avenue

755 Park Avenue

760 Park Avenue

815 Park Avenue

850 Park Avenue

876 Park Avenue

East Side

141 East 72nd Street

164 East 72nd Street

901 Madison Avenue

151 East 79th Street

108 East 86th Street

West End Avenue

588 West End Avenue

680 West End Avenue

749 West End Avenue

808 West End Avenue

Riverside Drive

270 Riverside Drive

276 Riverside Drive

West Side

161 West 86th Street

Downtown

23 Fifth Avenue

John E. Scharsmith

West Side

344 West 72nd Street

Mott B. Schmidt

Park Avenue

655 Park Avenue (with J. E. R. Carpenter)

1088 Park Avenue

East Side

19 East 72nd Street (with Rosario Candela)

Schultze & Weaver

Fifth Avenue

1215 Fifth Avenue

Schwartz & Gross

Fifth Avenue

912 Fifth Avenue

Park Avenue

67 Park Avenue

470 Park Avenue

525 Park Avenue

885 Park Avenue

888 Park Avenue

910 Park Avenue

911 Park Avenue

930 Park Avenue

941 Park Avenue

970 Park Avenue

983 Park Avenue

1045 Park Avenue

1070 Park Avenue

1085 Park Avenue

1095 Park Avenue

1111 Park Avenue

1125 Park Avenue

1165 Park Avenue

1185 Park Avenue

East Side

74–76 Madison Avenue

128 Central Park South

325 East 57th Street

130 East 75th Street

175 East 79th Street

180 East 79th Street

64 East 86th Street

103 East 86th Street

Central Park West

55 Central Park West

88 Central Park West

91 Central Park West

101 Central Park West

241 Central Park West

271 Central Park West

315 Central Park West

336 Central Park West

Riverside Drive

37 Riverside Drive

90 Riverside Drive

155 Riverside Drive

180 Riverside Drive

210 Riverside Drive

370 Riverside Drive

404 Riverside Drive

435 Riverside Drive

440 Riverside Drive

445 Riverside Drive

448 Riverside Drive

460 Riverside Drive

800 Riverside Drive

West End Avenue

255 West End Avenue

260 West End Avenue

290 West End Avenue

300 West End Avenue

375 West End Avenue

378 West End Avenue

420 West End Avenue

440 West End Avenue

500 West End Avenue

525 West End Avenue

574 West End Avenue

600 West End Avenue

650 West End Avenue

666 West End Avenue

700 West End Avenue

740 West End Avenue

771 West End Avenue

777 West End Avenue

845 West End Avenue

890 West End Avenue

924 West End Avenue

949 West End Avenue

West Side

19 West 69th Street

116 West 72nd Street

253 West 72nd Street

269 West 72nd Street

150 West 79th Street

157 West 79th Street

307 West 79th Street

324 West 84th Street

353 West 85th Street

156 West 86th Street

176 West 87th Street

610 West 110th Street

606 West 116th Street

Downtown

1 East 10th Street

55 East 11th Street

30 Fifth Avenue

44 Gramercy Park North

Segal & Sohn

Downtown

170 2nd Avenue

Sloan & Nast

Park Avenue

898 Park Avenue

Sloan & Robertson

Park Avenue

895 Park Avenue

East Side

1 Beekman Place

Herman M. Sohn

West Side

175 West 73rd Street

Starrett & Van Vleck

Fifth Avenue

820 Fifth Avenue

I. N. Phelps Stokes

Fifth Avenue

953 Fifth Avenue

W. E. D. Stokes

West Side

2109 Broadway (with Paul E. M. Duboy)

Sugarman & Berger

East Side

205 East 78th Street

25 East 86th Street

425 East 86th Street

40 East 88th Street

17 East 96th Street

Central Park West

239 Central Park West

262 Central Park West

West End Avenue

685 West End Avenue

Riverside Drive

310 Riverside Drive (with Helmle, Corbett & Harrison)

340 Riverside Drive

West Side

433 West 34th Street

51 West 86th Street

250 West 94th Street

207 West 106th Street

245 West 107th Street

Downtown

1 Fifth Avenue (with Helmle, Corbett & Harrison)

45 Fifth Avenue

31 East 12th Street

102 East 22nd Street

Sugarman, Hess & Berger

Park Avenue

935 Park Avenue

West End Avenue

365 West End Avenue

595 West End Avenue

Andrew J. Thomas

East Side

115 East 67th Street

Thomas & Wilson

Central Park West

227 Central Park West

Townsend Steinle & Haskell

Central Park West

151 Central Park West

West End Avenue

425 West End Avenue

640 West End Avenue

Riverside Drive

190 Riverside Drive

194 Riverside Drive

West Side

105–109 West 78th Street

Downtown

35 West 9th Street

Clarence True

West Side

1 West 89th Street

William Tuthill

Riverside Drive

355 Riverside Drive

Van Wart & Wein

Downtown

1 Christopher Street

40 Fifth Avenue (with McKim, Mead & White)

2 West 11th Street

D. Everett Waid

West End Avenue

465 West End Avenue

Warren & Wetmore

Fifth Avenue

856 Fifth Avenue

927 Fifth Avenue

960 Fifth Avenue (with Rosario Candela)

990 Fifth Avenue (with Rosario Candela)

1020 Fifth Avenue

Park Avenue

270 Park Avenue

280–290 Park Avenue

300–310 Park Avenue

320–330 Park Avenue

340–350 Park Avenue

400 Park Avenue

420–430 Park Avenue

903 Park Avenue (with Robert T. Lyons)

West Side

171 West 57th Street

James E. Ware

West Side

205 West 57th Street

H. Hobart Weekes

West Side

225 West 86th Street

Arthur Weiser

West End Avenue

263 West End Avenue

Henry W. Wilkinson

Central Park West

41 Central Park West

York & Sawyer

Fifth Avenue

660 Fifth Avenue

Park Avenue

860 Park Avenue

SELECTED BUILDINGS
BY LOCATION

Upper East Side: Fifth Avenue

810	J. E. R. Carpenter
820	Starrett & Van Vleck
825	J. E. R. Carpenter
2 East 64th Street	Rosario Candela
834	Rosario Candela
856	Warren & Wetmore
2 E67th	Rosario Candela
875	Emery Roth
880	Emery Roth
2 East 70th Street	Rosario Candela
907	J. E. R. Carpenter
912	Schwartz & Gross
920	J. E. R. Carpenter
927	Warren & Wetmore
930	Emery Roth
944	Nathan Korn
950	J. E. R. Carpenter
952	H. O. Chapman
953	I. N. Phelps Stokes
955	Rosario Candela
956	Nathan Korn
960	Rosario Candela/Warren & Wetmore
965	Margon & Holder
969	Joseph L. Raimist
988	J. E. R. Carpenter
990	Rosario Candela/Warren & Wetmore
993	Emery Roth

998	McKim, Mead & White
1010	Frederick F. French
1016	John B. Peterkin
1020	Warren & Wetmore
1030	J. E. R. Carpenter
1035	J. E. R. Carpenter
1040	Rosario Candela
1060	J. E. R. Carpenter
1067	Cass P. H. Gilbert
1068	Pennington, Lewis & Mills
1107	Rouse & Goldstone
1115	J. E. R. Carpenter
1120	J. E. R. Carpenter
1125	Emery Roth
1133	Emery Roth
1136	George F. Pelham
1140	Frederick F. French
1148	Walter B. Chambers
1150	J. E. R. Carpenter
1158	C. Howard Crane &Kenneth Franzheim
1165	J. E. R. Carpenter
1170	J. E. R. Carpenter
1200	Emery Roth

Upper East Side: Park Avenue

417	Emery Roth
455	Emery Roth
470	Schwartz & Gross

480	Emery Roth
485	Unknown
510	F. H. Dewey & Co.
520	William Boring
521	William Boring
525	Schwartz & Gross
535	Herbert Lucas
540	William Boring
550	J. E. R. Carpenter
555	George & Edward Blum
563	Walter B. Chambers
565	Robert T. Lyons
570	Emery Roth
575	George F. Pelham
580	J. E. R. Carpenter
610	J. E. R. Carpenter
620	J. E. R. Carpenter
625	J. E. R. Carpenter
630	J. E. R. Carpenter
635	J. E. R. Carpenter
640	J. E. R. Carpenter
655	J. E. R. Carpenter/Mott B. Schmidt
660	York & Sawyer
720	Cross & Cross/Rosario Candela
730	Hoffman & Goldstone
740	Rosario Candela
755	Rouse & Goldstone
760	Rouse & Goldstone
765/775	Rosario Candela
770	Rosario Candela
778	Rosario Candela
784	Emery Roth
791	George & Edward Blum
800	Electus D. Litchfield/Pliny Rogers
812	J. E. R. Carpenter
815	Rouse & Goldstone
820	Harry Allen Jacobs
823/829	Pickering & Walker
830	George & Edward Blum
840	George & Edward Blum
850	Rouse & Goldstone
860	York & Sawyer
863	Pollard & Steinem
875	George & Edward Blum
876	Rouse & Goldstone
885	Schwartz & Gross
888	Schwartz & Gross
891	Arthur Paul Hess
895	Sloan & Robertson
898	John Sloan & Adolph Nast
903	Robert T. Lyons/Warren & Wetmore
910	Schwartz & Gross
911	Schwartz & Gross
925	Delano & Aldrich
929	George & Edward Blum
930	Schwartz & Gross
935	Sugarman, Hess & Berger
940	George & Edward Blum
941	Schwartz & Gross
944	George F. Pelham

950	J. E. R. Carpenter
955	Robert T. Lyons
960	J. E. R. Carpenter
969	Pickering & Walker
970	Schwartz & Gross
975	Jacob M. Felson
983	Schwartz & Gross
993	Robert T. Lyons
1000	Emery Roth
1009	Emery Roth
1021	Rosario Candela
1035	Henry C. Pelton
1040	Delano & Aldrich
1045	Schwartz & Gross
1049	Arthur Paul Hess
1050	J. E. R. Carpenter
1060	J. E. R. Carpenter
1070	Schwartz & Gross
1075	George & Edward Blum
1085	Schwartz & Gross
1088	Mott B. Schmidt
1095	Schwartz & Gross
1100	De Pace & Juster
1105	Rosario Candela
1111	Schwartz & Gross
1112	Emery Roth
1120	George F. Pelham
1125	Schwartz & Gross
1130	George F. Pelham Jr.
1133	Nathan Korn
1155	Robert T. Lyons
1160	George F. Pelham
1165	Schwartz & Gross
1172	Rosario Candela
1175	Emery Roth
1185	Schwartz & Gross
1192	Rosario Candela
1220	Rosario Candela
1225	George F. Pelham
1230	Gronenberg & Leuchtag
1235	Gronenberg & Leuchtag
1240	George F. Pelham

Around the Upper East Side

140 East 28th Street	Emery Roth
Tudor City	Fred F. French/H. Douglas Ives
1 Beekman Place	Sloan & Robertson
2 Beekman Place	Rosario Candela
435 East 52nd Street	Bottomley, Wagner & White
14 Sutton Place South	Rosario Candela
1 Sutton Place	Rosario Candela with Cross & Cross
4 Sutton Place	Rosario Candela with Cross & Cross
25 Sutton Place	Rosario Candela with Cross & Cross
30 Sutton Place	Rosario Candela with Peabody, Wilson & Brown
320 East 57th Street	George & Edward Blum
325 East 57th Street	Schwartz & Gross
340 East 57th Street	Rosario Candela
419 East 57th Street	George & Edward Blum
435 East 57th Street	Emery Roth
442 East 57th Street	Lafayette A. Goldstone

447 East 57th Street	Rosario Candela
30 East 60th Street	Emery Roth
133 East 64th Street	Kenneth Murchison
136 East 64th Street	George F. Pelham
40 East 66th Street	Rosario Candela
131–135 East 66th Street	Charles Platt
115 East 67th Street	Andrew J. Thomas
210 East 68th Street	George & Edward Blum
315 East 68th Street	George & Edward Blum
142/146 East 71st Street	George F. Pelham
19 East 72nd Street	Rosario Candela/Mott B. Schmidt
50 East 72nd Street	Lafayette A. Goldstone
55 East 72nd Street	Unknown
141 East 72nd Street	Rouse & Goldstone
160 East 72nd Street	Kenneth Murchison
164 East 72nd Street	Rouse & Goldstone
901 Madison Avenue	Rouse & Goldstone
145 East 73rd Street	J. E. R. Carpenter
135 East 74th Street	George F. Pelham
35 East 76th Street	Bien & Prince
79 East 79th Street	Electus D. Litchfield
151 East 79th Street	Rouse & Goldstone
156 East 79th Street	George & Edward Blum
170 East 79th Street	J. E. R. Carpenter
133 East 80th Street	Rosario Candela
151 East 80th Street	Emery Roth
115 East 82nd Street	J. E. R. Carpenter
129 East 82nd Street	Emery Roth
1 Gracie Square	Rosario Candela/William Lawrence Bottomley
25 East End Avenue	Cross & Cross
120 East End Avenue	Charles Platt
130 East End Avenue	Emery Roth
108 East 86th Street	Rouse & Goldstone
115 East 86th Street	George F. Pelham
430 East 86th Street	Jacob M. Felson
520/530 East 86th Street	Charles Platt
110 East 87th Street	Boak & Paris
12 East 88th Street	Rosario Candela
14 East 90th Street	J. E. R. Carpenter
4 East 95th Street	J. E. R. Carpenter
8 East 96th Street	Rosario Candela
17 East 96th Street	Sugarman, Hess & Berger
49 East 96th Street	Thomas W. Lamb
60 East 96th Street	Emery Roth
70 East 96th Street	Rosario Candela
19 East 98th Street	Rosario Candela

Upper West Side: Central Park West

25	Irwin S. Chanin
41	Henry Wilhelm Wilkinson
55	Schwartz & Gross
65	Emery Roth
70	Rich & Mathesius
75	Rosario Candela
88	Schwartz & Gross
91	Schwartz & Gross
101	Schwartz & Gross
115	Irwin S. Chanin/Jacques Delamarre
1 West 72nd Street	Henry J. Hardenbergh
135	Clinton & Russell

145–146	Emery Roth
151	Townsend, Steinle & Haskell
211	Emery Roth
225	Emery Roth
227	Thomas & Wilson
230	Nathan Korn
239	Sugarman & Berger
241	Schwartz & Gross
251	Mulliken & Moeller
257	Mulliken & Moeller
262	Sugarman & Berger
271	Schwartz & Gross
275	Emery Roth
285	Robert T. Lyons
1 West 89th Street	Clarence True
293	Neville & Bagge
295	Emery Roth
300	Margon & Holder with Emery Roth
315	Schwartz & Gross
320	Emery Roth
322	George & Edward Blum
325	George F. Pelham
327	Nathan Korn
333	Robert J. Bodker
336	Schwartz & Gross
350	Jacob M. Felson
360	Rosario Candela

Upper West Side: West End Avenue

230	Rosario Candela
235	Gronenberg & Leuchtag
240	Rosario Candela
243	Emery Roth
246	J. E. R. Carpenter
255	Schwartz & Gross
260	Schwartz & Gross
263	Arthur Weiser
270	George F. Pelham
277	George & Edward Blum
290	Schwartz & Gross
300	Schwartz & Gross
310	Emery Roth
320	Rosario Candela
325	Neville & Bagge
333	Emery Roth
336	Boak & Paris
365	Sugarman, Hess & Berger
375	Schwartz & Gross
378	Schwartz & Gross
393	Goldner & Goldner
401	William B. Franke
420	Schwartz & Gross
425	Townsend, Steinle & Haskell
440	Schwartz & Gross
441	George F. Pelham
450	Boak & Paris
465	D. Everett Waid
470	George F. Pelham
473	Gaetano Ajello
490	Neville & Bagge

498	Neville & Bagge
500	Schwartz & Gross
505	Gaetano Ajello
512	Gaetano Ajello
515	Jacob M. Felson
522	Rosario Candela
525	Schwartz & Gross
530	Mulliken & Moeller
545	George F. Pelham
562	Walter Haefeli
574	Schwartz & Gross
575	Gaetano Ajello
580	Emery Roth
585	George F. Pelham
588	Rouse & Goldstone
590	Neville & Bagge
595	Sugarman, Hess & Berger
599	George & Edward Blum
600	Schwartz & Gross
601	Emery Roth
607	Rosario Candela
610	George & Edward Blum
617	George & Edward Blum
639	Gronenberg & Leuchtag
640	Townsend, Steinle & Haskell
645	Gaetano Ajello
650	Schwartz & Gross
666	Schwartz & Gross
670	George & Edward Blum
675	George F. Pelham
677	Leo F. Knust
680	Rouse & Goldstone
685	Sugarman & Berger
697	Jacob M. Felson
700	Schwartz & Gross
710	George F. Pelham
720	Emery Roth
736	Arthur Lobo
740	Schwartz & Gross
749	Rouse & Goldstone
755	Rosario Candela
760	George & Edward Blum
771	Schwartz & Gross
777	Schwartz & Gross
780	George & Edward Blum
782	Nast & Springsteen
789	Neville & Bagge
800	Rosario Candela
801	Neville & Bagge
808	Rouse & Goldstone
817	Neville & Bagge
820	Rosario Candela
825	Emery Roth
838	George & Edward Blum
845	Schwartz & Gross
875	Rosario Candela
878	Rosario Candela
884	Gaetano Ajello
885	Gaetano Ajello
890	Schwartz & Gross

895	Gaetano Ajello
900	Jacob M. Felson
905	Gaetano Ajello
910	George F. Pelham
915	Rosario Candela
924	Schwartz & Gross
945	Charles E. Birge
949	Schwartz & Gross

Upper West Side: Riverside Drive

5	Boak & Paris
33	George F. Pelham
37	Schwartz & Gross
50	Gronenberg & Leuchtag
52	Deutsch & Schneider
90	Schwartz & Gross
98	George F. Pelham
100	Boak & Paris
110	Gronenberg & Leuchtag
118	Gronenberg & Leuchtag
131	Neville & Bagge
137	Charles E. Birge
140	Emery Roth
150	Maurice Deutsch
155	Schwartz & Gross
160	Gaetano Ajello
173–175	J. E. R. Carpenter
180	Schwartz & Gross
186	Emery Roth
190	Townsend, Steinle & Haskell
210	Schwartz & Gross
230	H. Thomas O'Hara
243	Herman Lee Meader
258	William L. Rouse
270	Rouse & Goldstone
276	Rouse & Goldstone
280	Rosario Candela
285	Rosario Candela
290	George F. Pelham
299	Evan T. MacDonald
300	George F. Pelham
305	Lawlor & Haase
310	Helmle, Corbett & Harrison/Sugarman & Berger
315	Boak & Paris
340	Sugarman & Berger
355	Alfred C. Bossom/William Tuthill
360	Gaetano Ajello
370	Schwartz & Gross
375	Gaetano Ajello
380	William L. Rouse
390	Gaetano Ajello
395	Gaetano Ajello
404	Schwartz & Gross
410	Neville & Bagge
417	Denby & Nute
420	Gaetano Ajello
425	Rosario Candela
435	Schwartz & Gross
440	Schwartz & Gross
445	Schwartz & Gross

448	Schwartz & Gross
454	George & Edward Blum
460	Schwartz & Gross
800	Schwartz & Gross

Around the Upper West Side

30 Central Park South	J. E. R. Carpenter
112 Central Park South	J. E. R. Carpenter
1 West 67th Street	George Mort Pollard
40 West 67th Street	Rosario Candela
228 West 71st Street	Emery Roth
12 West 72nd Street	Emery Roth
253 West 72nd Street	Schwartz & Gross
305 West 72nd Street	Gaetano Ajello
170 West 73rd Street	Mulliken & Moeller
175 West 73rd Street	Herman M. Sohn
2109 Broadway	W. E. D. Stokes & Paul E. M. Duboy
161 West 75th Street	Rosario Candela
235 West 75th Street	Clinton & Russell
175 West 76th Street	Emery Roth
6-16 West 77th Street	Nathan Korn
20 West 77th Street	George F. Pelham
173 West 78th Street	George A. Bagge & Sons
2211 Broadway	Clinton & Russell
164 West 79th Street	George F. Pelham
307 West 79th Street	Schwartz & Gross
11 West 81st Street	Ditmars & Brite
15 West 81st Street	Emery Roth
25 West 81st Street	Gronenberg & Leuchtag
35 West 81st Street	Neville & Bagge
221 West 82nd Street	Emery Roth
222 West 83rd Street	Emery Roth
353 West 85th Street	Schwartz & Gross
5 West 86th Street	Boak & Paris
10 West 86th Street	George F. Pelham
40 West 86th Street	Jacob M. Felson
51 West 86th Street	Sugarman & Berger
107 West 86th Street	Jacob M. Felson
110 West 86th Street	Emery Roth
120 West 86th Street	George & Edward Blum
130 West 86th Street	Gronenberg & Leuchtag
140 West 86th Street	George F. Pelham
156 West 86th Street	Schwartz & Gross
161 West 86th Street	Rouse & Goldstone
200 West 86th Street	Margon & Holder
225 West 86th Street	Hiss & Weekes
257 West 86th Street	Pollard & Steinem
302 West 86th Street	Mulliken & Moeller
320 West 86th Street	Mulliken & Moeller
325 West 86th Street	Rosario Candela
334 West 86th Street	Rosario Candela
175 West 89th Street	Rosario Candela
201 West 89th Street	Emery Roth
205 West 89th Street	Charles Platt
304 West 89th Street	Rosario Candela
35 West 92nd Street	George G. Miller
215 West 92nd Street	Rosario Candela
220 West 93rd Street	Jacob M. Felson
250 West 94th Street	Sugarman & Berger
12 West 96th Street	Leo F. Knust

41 West 96th Street	Emery Roth
50 West 96th Street	George F. Pelham
306 West 100th Street	Unknown
314 West 100th Street	Unknown
210 West 101st Street	Emery Roth
245 West 104th Street	Gronenberg & Leuchtag
225 West 106th Street	Boak & Paris
315 West 106th Street	Rosario Candela
535 West 110th Street	Robert T. Lyons
610 West 110th Street	Schwartz & Gross
606 West 116th Street	Schwartz & Gross
1923 Seventh Avenue	Clinton & Russell

Downtown

56 Seventh Avenue South	Rosario Candela
10 Sheridan Square	Emery Roth
1 Christopher Street	Van Wart & Wein
45 Christopher Street	Emery Roth
136 Waverly Place	Unknown
1 University Place	Emery Roth
1 Fifth Avenue	Sugarman & Berger/Helmle, Corbett & Harrison
23 Fifth Avenue	Rouse & Goldstone
39 Fifth Avenue	Emery Roth
40 Fifth Avenue	McKim, Mead & White/Van Wart & Wein
41 Fifth Avenue	Rosario Candela
43 Fifth Avenue	Henry Anderson
45 Fifth Avenue	Sugarman & Berger
51 Fifth Avenue	Thomas W. Lamb
25 East 9th Street	Unknown
29-45 East 9th Street	Helmle & Corbett
28 East 10th Street	Emery Roth
40-50 East 10th Street	Helmle, Corbett & Harrison
164 Second Avenue	Emery Roth
170 Second Avenue	Segal & Sohn
2 West 11th Street	Van Wart & Wein
31 East 12th Street	Sugarman & Berger
59 West 12th Street	Emery Roth
299 West 12th Street	Emery Roth
302 West 12th Street	Boak & Paris
2 Horatio Street	Emery Roth
200 East 16th Street	Arthur Paul Hess
201 West 16th Street	Farrar & Watmaugh
242 East 19th Street	Emery Roth
81 Irving Place	George F. Pelham
34 Gramercy Park East	George DaCunha
36 Gramercy Park East	James Riely Gordon
44 Gramercy Park North	Schwartz & Gross
45 Gramercy Park North	George A. & Henry Boehm
60 Gramercy Park North	Emery Roth
1 Lexington Avenue	Herbert Lucas
4 Lexington Avenue	Grosvenor Atterbury
245 East 21st Street	Robert T. Lyons
301 East 21st Street	Jacob M. Felson
102 East 22nd Street	Unknown
235 East 22nd Street	George & Edward Blum
300 West 23rd Street	Emery Roth
405-465 West 23rd Street	Farrar & Watmaugh
470 West 24th Street	Farrar & Watmaugh

NOTES/BIBLIOGRAPHY

Notes

1. "A Peep into and a poke around 820 Fifth Avenue," The Real Estalker, http://realestalker.blogspot .com/2009/05/peep-into-and-poke-around-820 -fifth.html.
2. Max Abelson, "You're the Top!" *New York Observer*, May 1, 2007.
3. Sengdao Vongruksukdi, "Connecticut Home of Mysterious Heiress Huguette Clark for Sale," Newport Beach Real Estate, http://activerain .com/blogsview/2335859/connecticut-home-of- mysterious-heiress-huguette-clark-for-sale (June 6, 2011).
4. Christopher Gray, "A Majestic 1912 Apartment Tower for the Very Rich," *New York Times*, March 30, 2003.
5. Andrew Alpern, *Historic Manhattan Apartment Houses* (New York: Dover Publications, 1996).
6. "History of the Kress Collection," Kress Foundation, http://www.kressfoundation.org/collection/history/.
7. Wolfgang Saxon, "Evelyn Annenberg Jaffe Hall, Arts Patron, 93, Dies," *New York Times*, April 29, 2005.
8. Christopher Gray, "Streetscapes," *New York Times*, March 12, 1995.
9. "River House Round Up," The Real Estalker, http:// realestalker.blogspot.com/2010/12/river-house- round-up.html.
10. David Dunlap, "Irwin Chanin, Builder of Theaters and Art Deco Towers, Dies at 96," *New York Times*, February 26, 1988.
11. Steven Ruttenbaum, *Mansions in the Clouds: The Skyscraper Palazzi of Emery Roth* (New York: Balsam, 1986).
12. Christopher Gray, "Streetscapes/The Eldorado, at 90th Street; 1929 Art Deco Twin Towers on Central Park West," *New York Times*, December 9, 2001.
13. Christopher Gray, "Streetscapes/Mulliken & Moeller, Architects; Upper West Side Designs in Brick and Terra Cotta," *New York Times*, September 14, 2003.
14. Steven Gaines, "The Building of the Upper West Side," *New York* magazine, May 16, 2005.
15. Nora Ephron, "Moving On," *New Yorker*, June 5, 2006.
16. Laura L. Thorton, "The Belnord, 225 West 86th Street," *Architectural Ambler*, December 2009, http://www .architecturaltrust.org/images/documents/ambler _december2009web.pdf.
17. "Proposed Historic District Extension: 1 Lexington Avenue," Preserve2.org, http://www.preserve2.org/ gramercy/proposes/ext/ension/1lex.htm.

Bibliography

Alpern, Andrew. *Luxury Apartment Houses of Manhattan: An Illustrated History*. New York: Dover, 1993.
——. *The New York Apartment Houses of Rosario Candela and James Carpenter*. New York: Acanthus, 2001.
——. *New York's Fabulous Luxury Apartments*. New York: Dover, 1975.
Cromley, Elizabeth Collins. *Alone Together*. Ithaca: Cornell University Press, 1990.
Dolkart, Andrew S. *Morningside Heights*. New York: Columbia University Press, 1998.
Dolkart, Andrew S., and Susan Tunick. *George & Edward Blum*. New York: Friends of Terra Cotta Press, 1993.
Emporis website, www.emporis.com.
Gray, Christopher. *New York Streetscapes*. New York: Harry N. Abrams, 2003.
——. "Streetscapes/55 Central Park West; The Changing Colors of an Art Deco Landmark." *New York Times*, July 11, 1999.
——. "Streetscapes/89th Street and Broadway; In a 1916 Astor Building, a Private Garden Grows." *New York Times*, July 1, 2001.
——. "Streetscapes/770 and 778 Park Avenue, at 73rd Street; Fraternal-Twin Examples of East Side Superluxury." *New York Times*, June 8. 2003.
——. "Streetscapes: 780 West End Avenue; Making a Tall Building Taller." *New York Times*, May 14, 1989.
——. "Streetscapes/903 Park Avenue, at 79th Street; 1914 Apartment House Once Called World's Tallest." *New York Times*, May 12, 2002.
——. "Streetscapes/Mulliken & Moeller, Architects; Upper West Side Designs in Brick and Terra Cotta." *New York Times*, September 14, 2003.
——. "Streetscapes/Park Avenue and 79th Street: The Lack of Resemblance Is Completely Intentional." *New York Times*, March 14, 2009.
——. "Streetscapes/Park Avenue between 83rd and 84th Streets: Seven Apartment Houses in a Piazza-Like Setting." *New York Times*, March 9, 2008.
——. "Streetscapes/Readers' Questions; Architect's Legacies, a Mansion, an Early High-Rise." *New York Times*, September 5, 1999.
——. "Streetscapes/Seventh Avenue Between 15th and 16th Streets; Four 30's Apartment Buildings on 4 Chelsea Corners." *New York Times*, May 23, 2004.
——. "Streetscapes/The Colosseum and the Paterno, 116th Street and Riverside Drive; At Curves in the Road, 2 Unusually Shaped Buildings." *New York Times*, August 15, 1999.

——. "Streetscapes/West End Avenue; A Preservation Handbook in a Few Short Blocks." *New York Times*, June 24, 2007.
Hawes, Elizabeth. *New York, New York*. New York: Henry Holt, 1993.
Horsley, Carter. Building reviews for the website of CityRealty. www.cityrealty.com.
Kugel, Seth. "Taking a Peek at Prewar Classics." *New York Times*, July 9, 2006.
Mindlin, Alex. "A Bid to Shield a Row of Sturdy Soldiers." *New York Times*, May 18, 2008.
Mumford, Lewis. *Sidewalk Critic: Lewis Mumford's Writings on New York*. Edited by Robert Wojtowicz. New York: Princeton Architectural Press, 1998.
NYCityMap portal. http://gis.nyc.gov/doitt/mp/Portal.do.
Norton, Thomas E., and Jerry E. Patterson. *Living It Up*. New York: Atheneum, 1984.
Pennoyer, Peter, Anne Walker, and Robert A. M. Stern. *The Architecture of Warren & Wetmore*. New York: W. W. Norton, 2006.
Ruttenbaum, Steven. *Mansions in the Clouds: The Skyscraper Palazzi of Emery Roth*. New York: Balsam, 1986.
Stern, Robert A. M., Gregory Gilmartin, and John Massengale. *New York 1900: Metropolitan Architecture and Urbanism, 1890–1915*. New York: Rizzoli, 1983.
Stern, Robert A. M., Gregory Gilmartin, and Thomas Mellins. *New York 1930: Architecture and Urbanism between the Two World Wars*. New York: Rizzoli, 1987.
Trager, James. *Park Avenue; Street of Dreams*. New York: Atheneum, 1990.
——. *West of Fifth*. New York: Atheneum, 1987.
Wedemeyer, Dee. "Bing & Bing Sells Off Its Properties." *New York Times*, June 30, 1985.
White, Norval, and Elliot Willensky. *AIA Guide to New York City: The Classic Guide to New York's Architecture*. 5th ed. New York: Oxford University Press, 2010.

Published by
Princeton Architectural Press
37 East Seventh Street
New York, New York 10003

Visit our website at www.papress.com.

Project editor: Sara E. Stemen
Image research: Meredith Baber
Designer: Elana Schlenker

Special thanks to: Mariam Aldhani, Sara Bader, Nicola Bednarek Brower, Janet Behning,
Megan Carey, Carina Cha, Andrea Chlad, Barbara Darko, Benjamin English,
Russell Fernandez, Will Foster, Jan Hartman, Jan Haux, Diane Levinson, Jennifer Lippert,
Amrita Marino, Katharine Myers, Lauren Palmer, Jay Sacher, Rob Shaeffer, Andrew Stepanian,
Marielle Suba, Paul Wagner, and Joseph Weston of Princeton Architectural Press
—Kevin C. Lippert, publisher

Library of Congress Cataloging-in-Publication Data
Lynch, Geoffrey, 1970- author.
Manhattan classic : New York's finest prewar apartments / Geoffrey Lynch ;
principal photography by Evan Joseph and Mike Tauber.
    pages cm
Includes bibliographical references.
ISBN 978-1-61689-167-1 (alk. paper)
1. Apartment houses—New York (State)—New York—History—19th century. 2. Apartment
houses—New York (State)—New York—History—20th century. 3. Manhattan (New York,
N.Y.)—Buildings, structures, etc. 4. New York (State)—Buildings, structures, etc. I. Joseph,
Evan, illustrator. II. Tauber, Mike, illustrator. III. Title.
NA7862.N5L96 2014
728ʹ.314097471—dc23
                    2013026825

Image Credits

Anastassios Mentis Photography: 28–29, 62, 102
Bartomeu Amengual: Front of jacket, 63–65
Bilyana Dimitrova: 167–69
Emily Gilbert (photographer)/Fawn Galli Interiors (interior designer)/
    Romaine Orthwein: 188–91
Evan Joseph: Back of jacket, 2, 31–35, 36–42, 46–49, 52–53, 56–57, 71, 73,
    75–78, 80–81, 87–90, 93–95, 110–11, 113, 118–21, 123–25, 128–31, 134,
    142, 158–61, 164–65, 170–71, 173, 178–83, 186–87, 194, 196, 197
Fabio Carli: 103, 108–9
Geoffrey Lynch: Exterior photograph accompanying each building's
    name, 166
John M. Hall: 19–21
Michael Weinstein for MWSTUDIO: 98–101, 198–99
Mike Tauber: 17, 22–27, 54–55, 58–61, 67–69, 72, 97, 104, 184, 193, 200–3
Nico Arellano: 114–17
Tom Sibley: 50–51, 92
VHT Studios/Al Siedman: 195
VHT Studios/Andrew Kiracofe: 74
VHT Studios/Brett Beyer: 112, 126 right, 127, 162, 192
VHT Studios/Carl Wooley: 105
VHT Studios/Caryn Posnansky: 91, 146, 147 top
VHT Studios/Elizabeth Dooley: 43, 145
VHT Studios/Laura Dante: 143, 185
VHT Studios/Martha Thorneloe: 79, 85, 126 left, 172
VHT Studios/Melanie Green: 135, 137
VHT Studios/Scott Wintrow: 70, 148, 152, 154–55
VHT Studios/Terry Morales: 138–39, 147 bottom, 163, 174–75
VHT Studios/Tina Gallo: 136, 149–51, 153